We Are the Creators

A Little Everyday Philosophy

L. R. Sumpter

OZARK
MOUNTAIN
PUBLISHING

© 2015 L.R. Sumpter
2nd Printing 2016

For permission, serialization, condensation, adaptions, or for our catalog of other publications, write to Ozark Mountain Publishing, LLC., P.O. Box 754, Huntsville, AR 72740, ATTN: Permissions Department.

Library of Congress Cataloging -in-Publication Data

Sumpter, L.R. 1943

We Are The Creators by L.R. Sumpter

This is a positive message about your soul's power, your life's purpose, NDE's (Near Death Experiences), déjà vu and your spiritual guides.

1. Metaphysics 2. Manifestation/Creation 3. NDEs (Near Death Experiences) 4. Spirit Guides

I. Sumpter, L.R. 1943 II. Metaphysics III. Manifestation/Creation IV. Title

Library of Congress Catalog Card Number: 2015942707

ISBN: 9781940265117

Cover Art and Layout: www.noir33.com
Book set in: Lucida Sans, Segoe Print
Book Design: Tab Pillar
Published by:

PO Box 754

Huntsville, AR 72740

WWW.OZARKMT.COM

Printed in the United States of America

This book and this entire project are dedicated to my wife, Judith, who steered me into these interests and encouraged me to write about them. Her support and that of family and friends have been of critical importance to the progress of this book.

Endorsements

If the unseen spiritual world has been filled with mysteries, Lee Sumpter has discovered captivating and intriguing insight and study with his newest book, "We are the Creators"! The interesting content will confirm thoughts and beliefs you have always had and will unlock so many doors of understanding. Author Sumpter gives us practical principles and practices to draw from in applying them to today's world. I look forward to more books from Lee, and have enjoyed his past articles tremendously! I highly recommend this book! "We Are the Creators" will make your brain sizzle and spark!

Donna Abner RN, CFGM
Spiritual Consultant
Retired Vangent Operations Manager

As an artist and painting instructor, I have seen that people of all ages have a need to channel their energy into creative outlets. Encompassing a multitude of art forms from the most expensive paints and brushes to whatever is at their disposal, they strive for this with a sense of purpose that will not be denied. Lee Sumpter shines a light on how and why we create – a truly thought provoking book.

Lucie LeBeau– artist

"We Are the Creators is a fascinating and essential guide to finding peace, health and happiness through the process of discovery. In the old adage of 'If all else fails, read the instructions,' herein lies the excellent explanations within the instructions. On our journey from Clod to God, many experiences are offered for our growth. Within this study, there are 'Aha!' moments of enlightenment in every chapter written in a modern, clear and enjoyable manner. Enjoy the journey. Life is all about the journey."

Dr. Richard LeBeau, artist and teacher

"A new and clear Channel has appeared on the horizon of lightworkers. L.R. Sumpter's willingness to allow his gift to the earth in the form of this book is a blessing to us all. In the midst of earthly and cosmic turmoil, the wisdom of this information will feed your soul as you resonate with these truths."

Nancy S. Jones
Certified Spiritual Counselor with the
American Board of Hypnotherapy

Contents

Introduction

Halfway through my first year of retirement from a thirty-five-year teaching career, I began to write what I thought was a series of essays in an effort to help friends and relatives who were suffering from prostate cancer. I believe that one major cause of prostate cancer is the approach of post middle age. I think that most men approaching this point in their life begin to ask themselves, "What am I going to do?" In my essays I wanted to explain to my male friends and relatives, that even though they were approaching a time in their life of perhaps diminishing responsibilities, they were still doing many very important things to maintain their world. I wanted to explain just how powerful the soul is, that their soul was in fact literally creating their world, so they could have whatever world they wanted. In other words, I wanted to point out that instead of experiencing diminishing powers, they were far more powerful than they ever imagined, and there were lots of things that they could do such as changing the weather instead of just talking about it.

As I launched into this project I determined to explain just how exactly we make our own world. This sent me back into an area of studies that I began in my early youth: phenomenology and metaphysics. At about this time, I was afflicted with a series of mildly painful kidney stones, which kept me confined to an area proximate to medical help. Purely on a whim and to find out what may lie ahead of me in my retirement, I consulted a reader of the Akashic records, about which I was really pretty skeptical. I was told that instead of just essays, I was writing a book. This book was to be about choices that would lead to a new awareness of spiritual powers, and I had a certain rather short time frame in which this book was to be finished. I had an unstated deadline! I had hoped to go on a fishing trip instead of all this. I promptly consulted another psychic friend of mine who had previously explained to me that I had kind souls who acted as guides and helped me with my teaching. She confirmed that, yes, these kind souls expected me to write a book that would be completed in about eight months. I never did ask, "Eight months from when?" One simple reason that I did not ask was that I did not believe that I could actually write a book. When I began to object to this insistence from the spiritual world, I was further informed that it had been decided by my guides, or someone in the world of spirit, that I had just the right life experience, and that I had done just the right philosophical studies to explain what they wanted explained. Additionally beneficial, they explained, were the years of suffering through an insecure and chaotic life lived all over the world and the fact that I was a teacher of English and other languages. I was the perfect candidate, it seemed. Just to make sure that I got to work, the problems with the kidney stones lasted about six weeks and pretty much kept me confined to a recliner.

I was puzzled by the suggestion that this book was about choices, but I had dabbled with writing all of my life, and I had been a teacher of writing, and I definitely wanted to help those who were suffering from prostate cancer. I guess I just muddled on in a state of wonder. However, little by little, ideas would come into my head that surprised me, and I began to tackle once again my lifelong curiosity about just how we relate to our world and vice versa. The more I reviewed my studies and the more I tried to write about them, the more new ideas came to me. At first I revolted about these new ideas, sometimes for weeks. I found them preposterous and contrary to our established and accepted understanding of how things are in the world. Eventually the necessary arguments and examples from my own experience came into my mind and I acquiesced. These ideas became the foundation blocks for a radically new way to understand reality and specifically how we create it. The more I understood, the more I accepted.

Finally, one morning while I was standing at the entryway to the kitchen of our vacation home, I became aware of someone standing just behind me to my left. It was a little startling. My wife was in the kitchen in front of me. No one had entered our little lakeshore home. I spun around to see what or who it was and got a quick glimpse of a short, very stocky blond woman with short hair who was dressed in a sort of powder-blue and white tunic something like I had seen on statues of Roman slaves. She also wore an elaborate and sparkly belt and an array of shiny necklaces. I got a glimpse of some sort of sandals on her feet. She had a definite air of dignity and purpose about her, as if it were the most natural thing in the world that she would be standing there where there was a wall and a sofa. In a split second, the image evaporated but not my riotous emotions.

I would not rest until, with trembling hands, I got my psychic friend on the cell phone. I described my experience to her. She said that the whole story made her shiver, but she explained that the short blond woman, that she too could see, was a new guide who had been brought in to the project to help out with certain parts that were more difficult. Little by little I got a name, Feh, and the explanation that she came from an Earth life a very long time ago when the Earth had an axis that was almost ninety degrees different from what it is now. She had lived approximately in what is now called the Middle East, but that then it was neither middle nor east. More details were also provided.

Now, when I recovered from my shock, my writing plunged into ideas that I *really* revolted against, and I refused to include them. More examples and arguments would come into my mind, and I began to see the world in even more new ways. Finally, once again, I agreed to proceed.

Sometimes for page after page, a new voice would take over in my words and sentences, and notions entirely beyond my imagination would flow out onto the pages. Some sentences that would come to me were actually direct answers to questions or objections that I would have to the things that I was learning. Sometimes, after several hours of this kind of composition, I would be utterly exhausted and unable to do much of anything else. At that time more than a year ago, I would never have imagined that I would be willing to tell this story; much less organize all of this into a useful book.

I am aware that there were other inspirational voices that helped me with my work. I have learned the names of most of them. Most of the time, I knew that I was being guided by a composite voice that had no particular source. Sometimes I was well aware by the tone and cadence that a particular source was guiding me. And, then, sometimes I was composing sentences on my own from my own studies and observations over the years.

To sum it all up, the first two chapters and the chapter on déjà vu are mostly all from me. So are the chapter on our physical senses and most of the final two chapters. The intervening chapters have many arguments that I hammered out in order to explain what I was coming to understand better and better, but the basic propositions about material manifestations of our life plan are as startling to me as they will probably be to many readers, and they definitely did not originate in my thinking. Many of these ideas are very old but have been forgotten or neglected or suppressed. Many of them have come out in other places in different forms. I know that I have been guided to such ideas by reading books such as Jane Roberts's *Seth Speaks*, Ruth Montgomery's books, and Sylvia Brown's books. Wayne Dyer's books and televised talks have definitely inspired me to keep asking the questions that have led to the answers that I feel are a large part of this book. However, I feel that some ideas came to me literally "out of the blue."

These ideas have, little by little, made me feel much more in control of my life and much freer. They have allowed me to comfortably shed many negative thoughts from both Western and Eastern cultures that I always felt were stultifying. Ideas such as original sin and the subservience of women in Judeo-Christian thought, and the necessity to abandon desire and aspirations in Hindu-Buddhist traditions have easily evaporated into historical obsolescence. Instead, I feel like I have a positive place in human history along with billions of other people. I feel like we are solidly united in our endeavors, that we are beginning to create a whole new world for the Earth, and that we have power beyond our wildest imaginations. I hope that you, the reader, will feel this way too.

Chapter 1

Just Look at What We Have Done!

The purpose of this book is to convince each and every one of you that you are intelligent and powerful beyond your wildest imaginings. It is meant to reveal to you all of the amazing things that your intelligence is doing in each moment of your life. It will reveal how a lot of the things that you think you are using your intelligence to do, such as planning your day, are not as important as they seem. This book is meant to open your eyes to the many things that your consciousness or your soul is busy doing to create the reality of your life experience. All of this information will not necessarily change what you have to do each moment of each day, but hopefully it will radically change your attitude toward what you are doing and who you are. It will free you to be even more creative than you already are and open new possibilities in your life that are right before your very nose.

To begin this new look at human consciousness we will pick an arbitrary date in recent history: about 1750, give or take fifty years, will do. There is nothing special about this particular year. It is just that we must begin somewhere in the fairly recent past. What is important here is to contrast the accomplishments of humankind in the last 250 to 300 years with the accomplishments of the last 2,000 to 10,000 years and beyond.

The first major change from life in the last 10,000 or so years is the appearance of a democratically organized country on the North American continent that had no king. Not only that, but each of the original thirteen states that agreed to form this political organization was governed by an electorate and all of the subsequent thirty-seven states which joined the union in later years were governed the same way with no monarch.

From roughly 1775 on, fifty new states in North America and about the same number around the world were formed without a king. At various times, many states reverted back to dictatorial forms of government, but the idea of the king as god or king by divine right has faded rapidly from modern political organization. By contrast, as far back as we look in known history, either recorded or legendary, there have been kings, queens, princes, and princesses. Now after thousands of years, we organize ourselves around the consent of the governed. And the people giving this consent, the voters, are typically educated in ways never before seen in recorded history. One result of this democratic political system is that in the vast territories of the American continents and in Europe, nations are no longer fighting each other because someone is seen as "the other"; that is, as somehow different and therefore threatening. Many cultural differences still exist among the people who inhabit these lands, but they do not fight among themselves.

The next major change in human organization that comes about after 1750 is the Industrial Revolution. There are many important developments from the Industrial Revolution that will be discussed soon, but the primary development in human organization is the factory, especially factories powered by steam engines. This power source, which was later replaced by internal combustion engines and electricity, allowed factories to be located away from watercourses or wherever it was convenient. These factories were also a complete alteration of human existence. Family and village units for the production of goods were replaced by huge and complex manufacturing centers where work and life became as mechanical as the machinery. Everyone lived by the clock, a mechanical time-measuring device, instead of by the sun. The rhythms of nature were largely abandoned. However, assembly-line-produced goods, such as Henry Ford's Model T automobile, were now available to the masses.

For thousands of years, only the few nobles and their families, along with successful merchant families, could afford much more than bare necessities. Factory-produced goods and factory wages made things available to everyone where, in the past, they had only been available to a few.

Around 1804, the steam engine was improved to the point that it not only could pump water and power factories, but it was put to use to transport people and goods on rails. This was done in England. Only about sixty-five years later people and goods were being moved across the oceans and the North American continent by steam power. It was now possible to travel across the western United States in two weeks instead of three months.

In the same time frame of 1800 to 1865 instant communications over great distances also became possible with the invention of the telegraph in 1844 by Samuel F. B. Morse, after many years of effort by dozens of others. Morse's telegraph used electricity generated by chemical batteries, a very old technology, but by 1881 electricity was available from central generation stations in some places. Central power generation went hand-in-hand with the lightbulb, which allowed factories and other activities to go on all night. Over still another set of wires went the human voice by telephone in 1877. Thirty years later images went over the wires by means of the television; and in thirty more years, around 1907, voice and imagery moved without wires!

In just the hundred years from 1800 to 1900 thousands of years of limitations to human communication posed by space and time were wiped out. Business could be carried out by people all over the world across oceans and mountain ranges. The world was much more tied together.

In 1776 when the Declaration of Independence was being signed, communication over some distance was accomplished by writing on paper or sheepskin, which was then carried to its destination by man or beast. This was the norm for thousands of years. One hundred years later in 1876, people could actually speak to each other over great distances, even across the world. In a few more years this communication could be carried out with no physical connection between the speakers!

Another remarkable thing about this blindingly rapid change from the ancient to the modern is that the early versions of telephones were rather complicated. Some had seven wires. Generators had to be cranked; bells had to be rung; speakers and receivers had to be used in various forms. Nevertheless, just as people do today, the devices were quickly applied to personal and commercial use; and just like today, people in the 1900s managed all of the complicated gadgetry. Imagine someone from the 1300s adjusting the spark and the gas and cranking a Model T to get it started. How many of us had a crystal radio set? The old black-and-white movies of women in leg-of-mutton dresses and mustachioed men in top hats using telephones, cranking automobile engines, and inventing names for gadgets and newly discovered elements is incongruous, but it happened rapidly enough. The people who lived in the midst of this rapid change seemed to have an innate ability to adapt and to learn just like people now.

At the same time that rapid change in communication was occurring, similarly revolutionary changes were occurring in transportation. At about the same time transcontinental steam-powered railroads were being built, gasoline and diesel engines were being created. In 1879, there were gasoline engines, and by 1897, there were diesel engines. Only thirty years after that, in 1927, a jet engine was being tested.

In just two hundred years we have opened up the very essence of nature for our own use. Between 1750 and 1850, wood and coal were the power source for rapidly improving steam engines, which are *external* combustion engines. Then petroleum products began to be the power source for *internal* combustion engines, including jet engines. By 1950, atomic power was used to power warships and to generate electricity. Burning wood, coal, or oil for light and heat had certainly been the practice for as long as anyone knows. To change from igniting hydrocarbons in the open air for heat and light to forcing hydrocarbons to combine with air in an enclosed space where the power released can be immediately applied is a big jump. To then split the very atoms of matter to obtain power is beyond imagination when that imagination only recently was limited to a world of taking things just as they are in nature.

In the same two hundred years, we have changed from getting about on land and sea using what nature provided in the way of motive power, such as animals, wind or water, or other humans, to being able to fly about the Earth or across it using the internal chemical processes of nature. Really we have externalized the internal. The wires that send electricity so that we can communicate with each other or power our motors are similar to the nerve ganglions in our bodies that send electrical signals from our brains to our muscles. The internal combustion engine mimics the way that muscle cells oxidize carbohydrates in our bodies to obtain power and heat. Atomic power is an extension of this process and is based upon the way we create new living cells in our bodies! We have in two hundred or so years brought our internal power and communication processes out into the external world. The similarity of computers to the human brain or any brain was instantly recognized. Along with computers, that are like simplified brains, we have replicated our eyes, our ears, our ability to speak, our ability to smell, to touch, and our ability to record experience in our memory. We can even project the products of our imaginations on screens and send them around the world for others to see and know. We can even record the presence of extrasensory energy such as x-rays, ultraviolet, ultrasound, and infrared, and we can use these to see into our bodies, other matter, or to see in the dark.

Not only have we externalized the internal and made the heretofore unknown known, we have reached a point where the composition of material reality can be penetrated from any angle that seems convenient. We are more familiar with our created world. We have more minerals, more forms of energy, and more new compounds than in the past. We are even creating new materials like plastics or carbon fiber that did not exist in nature.

We have created a whole new world almost instantly. In 1775 our ancestors were leading pack animals through Cumberland Gap into the fabled bluegrass region of Kentucky. In 1969, just 194 years later, we, their descendants, sent astronauts to the moon. In 1969, when Neil Armstrong was taking his first step on the moon, there were people living who could recall seeing their first automobile and airplane. There is no known equivalent jump in human capabilities in the previous 10,000 years. In geologic time, 200 to 250 years is immeasurable; in archaeology, it is maybe a nanosecond!

Up to 1,700 years after the appearance of Jesus of Nazareth in what is now Israel, there were no such inventions, conveniences, or transportation or communications systems such as we enjoy today. Only in the last 250 years or so has the world been united in its ability to communicate and provide anything to anyone anywhere. How many millennia do we now need to add in order to see this as a major break in the historical continuity of human intellectual and technical capabilities?

In addition to the proliferation of ever more capable and complicated gadgets, everything is speeded up. It is now possible to get things done with blinding speed. Buildings get built in days or weeks instead of years. It only takes seconds to manufacture some very sophisticated consumer products. Even our children seem to be growing up faster! The sudden acceleration of creativity in matter and energy of the last 250 years has not slowed. We pay little attention to this change since we are in the midst of it. We are being carried along by it. In fact, it is because of all the changes in information availability that we can mark out both when these changes started to happen in recent history and what their course may be in human affairs.

We live in expectation of more change and more innovation. We accept that this is an ongoing process. This is not where we are today or for the last ten years. It is the way things are at this instant. In another instant, someone somewhere in the world will change it. Our entire world is in a process of dynamic change. We are all part of this change. We readily accept the new changes and new gadgets as they come along. Our children accept them even more readily than those of us who watched the gadgets appear. The miraculous has become commonplace. And this is the case for all of us. Think of the turbaned Tuareg with a satellite phone or women in black chadors watching television. Cell phones are everywhere, even where there are few roads. We are all suddenly a new kind of being. We know new stuff, we can do new stuff, and we expect new stuff to appear any minute.

In the two hundred years or so since the beginning of the Industrial Revolution, we have created the ability to move ourselves, our thoughts, and our goods and services about the world with unprecedented rapidity. In the process of creating this capability we have created external equivalents to most of our human capabilities. Our copper and aluminum wires imitate our nerve ganglions; our internal combustion engines provide power in the same way that our cells power our muscles and organs. In splitting atoms for atomic power, we have externalized the way that our cells make new flesh for our organs. We can project our thoughts and images on screens, project them around the world, and store them in memory devices. We have cameras to see, microphones to hear, gas and odor sniffers to sniff, sensors for texture and tastes, and we are trying to put all of these things in robotic artificial bodies. We have brought about a new previously unseen system of governance, and we have brought peace where there was always war. We are showing signs of being some kind of new human being.

In the midst of these rapid innovations in the way people live on the Earth, there are many people whose thinking still revolves around ideas and beliefs that are centuries, even millennia old. Most of this thinking is based on old beliefs about who has the right to certain categories, certain types, of knowledge. Many of us in one way or another believe that certain kinds of knowledge and the capabilities that may come from that knowledge are forbidden. It is time to abandon such beliefs.

Chapter 2

We Need to Believe That We Can Do It

Now, have we been invaded by an alien force from some distant and very advanced civilization in space? Has someone appeared among us on several continents to teach us all of this hidden engineering? Since there is no clear and pervasive evidence for these two explanations, then we might conclude that all of this came from the spiritual realm. We know that inventors and other creative people speak of dreams and hunches as sources for their ideas, and we accept this readily. Where do these hunches and dreams come from?

We must now move to the intellectual point where we accept that we are aware of new sources of knowledge and a new mission different from past times. If we can take it for granted that some new technological feat will appear momentarily, why can't we take for granted the obvious spiritual source for this new thing? Why do we have to continue to fear social and religious consequences for expressing intuitive knowledge? How long will we allow ourselves to continue to fear the witch-hunting priests who seek to extirpate any challenge to their unique spiritual authority? Clearly this is an ancient fear. Oddly intuitive knowledge, such as $E = mc^2$ for example, that is expressed in mathematical and scientific terms, is free of this opprobrium and fear, at least in the West. The same knowledge expressed in private narrative, such as "My deceased grandmother appeared to me last night and warned me about this business deal," however, may run afoul of the established religious and academic authorities. Moreover, if knowledge travels instantly over the Internet, it is acceptable; if it travels instantly telepathically from mind to mind, it is considered freaky. Even though parts of Internet communication are wireless and certainly not entirely understood, this is more acceptable to most of us than purely mental communication.

We need to recognize the rapid advances made in spiritual awareness that correspond to the rapid advances in material creation. No doubt the material creation is a reflection of spiritual connectedness. In other words it is time that we realize that in fact we are capable of all of the things that we have done in the last two hundred or so years and that, therefore, we are indeed a new kind of spiritual being on Earth—all of us.

There is another kind of choice that we can make in our material existence and that is the one where we decide to bring all of our spiritual, nonmaterial experiences into the conscious everyday world. Why do we have to talk about ESP in hushed guarded tones? We all know someone who knows who is calling on the phone, or who is at the door, or who is coming to visit. How many people know when someone is sick or about to die? There are now television shows where communication with friends and family who have died is demonstrated and shows where communication with spiritual guides is discussed, but all of this still bears the stigma of weird. Each person, however, has the possibility of developing these abilities for themselves now.

Clearly miraculous developments are occurring anyway in the world. How much that is even more miraculous and beneficial might occur if we collectively recognize our spiritual existence, our power to create our world, and our purpose for being here in the first place? If we can bring so much that is hidden in matter and in the Earth out into our lives, then why can we not bring out the nonmaterial reality? Is it any less miraculous to create a laser beam to measure the land than it is to send healing or loving thoughts to someone in need? If we can use uranium ore to create various forms of power, why can't we use our spiritual powers consciously and intentionally to bring about beneficial changes in our lives and the lives of others?

Many accept without question that a church congregation or other group with common interests may pray together for someone's healing and recovery from an illness. These same groups also pray for beneficial outcomes to other life events. Why can it not be possible for everyone to exercise these powers for good in their everyday lives according to their knowledge and abilities? We accept readily the appearance of some new gadget in our world. Why can't we accept as readily a new spiritual "gadget?"

If we consider the material progress that our cultures have made in the last two hundred years, then it is proper to ask, "Where is the corresponding spiritual progress?" All we need to do is ask. Great spiritual power is available simply by acknowledging its existence. It is all there anyway, behind everything that happens in our lives. Once we are aware of the unlimited spiritual abilities that we all possess and use to do even the simplest daily tasks, then we can begin to apply these powers to bring about even greater benefit to ourselves, our families, and our societies. No one doubts that the gadgets could take over a large part of our daily existence. In many ways they already have! There are, however, spiritual gadgets that we use constantly to manage our lives of which we pretend to be unaware. Stop pretending! Our cultural beliefs allow us to accept a new computer or TV or cell phone where none existed a short time ago. Where did these things come from? Why didn't even powerful kings and emperors of a few hundred years ago have such things? Why is it that today a child can talk to someone on the other side of the world, when the most powerful monarch two hundred years ago couldn't even imagine such power? The same spiritual knowledge that brought about the creation of our modern gadgets can bring about new spiritual awareness for all. Our gadgets are in the form of solid matter that has weight and takes up space. Ideas are more powerful than any gadget, but they have no weight, nor do they take up space.

Those who live in functioning democracies experience every day the results of the powerful ideas of justice and freedom. They live in countries where these ideas are the foundation of their society. Is it such a jump in belief that these results could be available to everyone on Earth if only a large majority of people became united in this idea? Why should such an idea be any more difficult to accept than a new cell phone? In many ways the new cell phone is a step in the direction of freedom and justice for all, but everyone can certainly actively share these ideas without the cell phone.

Soon after the end of World War II, religious and political leaders promoted the idea that the various nations of Europe could stop fighting among themselves and live with a common purpose. Less than one hundred years later, that is the status quo of Europe. For thousands of years these various peoples have fought among themselves, even in the days of the Roman Empire! Now quite suddenly, that is no longer the case, and almost no one notices. Peace and cooperation are taken for granted as if they were always there. This is a miraculous and sudden change brought about by the introduction of powerful ideas at just the right time. These powerful ideas, with obviously beneficial results, can still bring about miraculous changes elsewhere. They must be moved from the realm of the unconscious to the conscious world. They must be made into conscious intent as they were in Europe. There can be more miracles. This is what spiritual power can do.

There have been a few problems with getting to a point where this is intellectually acceptable. As the eighteenth-century European philosophers considered a movement away from monarchical forms of government, and European people began a corresponding physical movement away from the continent to the New World, there were all kinds of experiments in social organization taken up both in Europe proper and on the American continents. Most of these experiments were based on one form or another of communal living. Many were based upon some commonly held religious convictions among the participants, but all were attempts to govern society by ways other than monarchy. When the actual rebellions occurred in the American colonies, the New World, then in France and later in the rest of Europe, everyone expected that a break with totalitarian social order would follow in perpetuity. However, the mania for dependence upon monarchical and religious control was very deeply seated in the human psyche. In fact, this mania was often carried by the experimenters and rebels in their religious organizations. Even though the 1700s saw this fundamental shift from the 10,000-or-more-year-old monarchical political order, the hold of dependence upon the control of religious authorities for everyday thinking and fundamental beliefs continued. Europeans on both continents—all the while that they were declaring their political independence—were still dependent upon religious traditions of central or priestly control whether emanating from Rome or elsewhere. All of this was considered to be in the natural order of things. Yes, there was a Protestant movement away from Catholicism, but this often took the form of substituting one source of control for another.

It was on the American frontier, where really a new kind of independent thinker was emerging, that it was possible to experiment with true mental and spiritual independence. On the frontier, religious or any other form of control was often far away. Besides, the frontiersmen and the original isolated settlers from the old world, such as Norsemen and Melungeons, often intermingled with the various groups of already present inhabitants whose beliefs were also necessarily not dictated by some distant authority. In this way, it was possible to be self-reliant with respect to what a person could do, could know, or could feel.

The American frontier provided the true environment for the ultimate experiment in spiritual and physical independence.

Catholic ritual processions marking religious holidays were of little use in impressing wolves, bears, and mountain lions with empty stomachs. The seven-day weekly cycle with confession, sermon, priestly ministrations, etc., could hardly have seemed adequate against the vast, silent wilderness and the imminent threat to self-preservation. Where the old order was advanced step by step as in the Spanish west or the French northeast, these forms of control were preserved effectively, but in many places far from the reach of these influences, new forms of thought were necessary for settlers of European origin.

These new forms of belief were, however, actually very old. They were forms that were and still are commonly enjoyed by the native peoples of the Americas. These beliefs found spiritual power in all things. Spiritual guidance was as much available from inner-seeking meditation as from observing the cycles of nature. There was no hierarchy of spiritual authority. There was no idea of the necessarily masculine voice of divine teachings. As is the case in the Far Eastern countries like China and Japan, knowledge of the divine was also available in a garden, forest, mountain, or prairie.

Nevertheless, self-reliance was the rule for the frontier. There were no tax collectors and no tithes for long stretches of time. Self-reliance was the rule with respect to both physical and spiritual success. As European civilization made its way westward in its many forms, it was invariably changed and restructured to meet the challenges of the frontier. Notable examples of these changes are the "lynch laws" with respect to horse thievery, marriage practices with the intermingling of cultures and religions, and the idea that the average person could own property and land. Along with this last idea went the ideas of caste and hereditary privilege. No doubt the freedom of peoples of European descent from the former ineluctable social and political structures brought about the release of tremendous energy into human enterprise. Where European civilization had been centuries in the making with untold wars, waste, and rigidity, the North American continent saw an equally powerful and successful civilization rise up in only about two hundred years. In about 1775, thousands of people were streaming through Cumberland Gap into Kentucky, on foot or on horseback. About two hundred years later, their descendants had spanned the continent by iron rail and hard-surfaced roads and had sent men to the moon.

No one gives much thought to all of this. A change in a social and political order that had prevailed for probably 10,000 years or perhaps many more comes about in less than two hundred years and no one notices! This is all taken for granted, but it is proof that something important is happening in human life. Now a corresponding change must occur in spiritual life. Political order based upon mutual consent is certainly revolutionary and liberating, but the power released by freedom to choose and explore one's own beliefs cannot yet be imagined.

Clearly the need for a spiritual authority outside of one's own mind is deeply established. Many countries have thrown off the yoke of monarchy only to put on one of dictatorship in some other form. At the beginning of the twentieth century a great disillusionment set in because it appeared to European minds as well as those in the Far East that the results of the shift from monarchy were a disaster. Not only did various dictators take the place of monarchs in the name of social justice, liberation, the uplifting of the downtrodden, etc., but these dictators promptly engaged the world in two world wars.

So profound was the disillusionment that many people declared that it was God that had brought about all of the misery and chaos. In a half-hearted attempt at intellectual independence from the thinking of the past, the assessment was that "If there was a God, then he was responsible." The rejection of past thinking had in fact gone so far as to declare that the idea of God, of the spiritual aspect of human experience, belonged to the religious institutions that had taken control of these ideas and that the end result of these ideas was the destruction brought on by two world wars. These thinkers had thrown the baby out with the bath water. It was not so easy to separate the malicious abuses of power over spiritual teachings from the power and benefits of the teachings themselves. Just as during the Second World War, many Catholic institutions tried to protect people from the horrors of the war while others did nothing or helped the oppressors; the Church itself was totally enmeshed in all that happened. The keepers of the concentration camps celebrated Christmas and took Communion.

From all of this, a type of cynicism has taken over modern human thinking, which is expressed in many forms. Immediately after the war, there was an intellectual rejection of all things religious in Europe which spread to the Americas. Any ideas from organized religion were suspect. As a substitute, a philosophy of humanism, existentialism, situation ethics, and relativism was accepted. According to this way of thinking, theft was not inherently bad. It all depended upon the context in which it occurred. During the wars, stealing from the enemy was certainly not bad, but good. Every moral weakness was justifiable according to the social milieu in which it manifested itself. Thievery, in a ghetto full of desperate people, was to be expected, even condoned. Nothing had any meaning. The world had gone to hell in a hand basket. It was foolish to put one's faith in anything or anyone. No human endeavor would ever produce a beneficial result. Everything that anyone set out to do was probably motivated by greed, etc.

Such has been the thinking. This is certainly a spiritual sickness, and it is a prevalent legacy of the beginnings of the last century. Another form of this thinking is that people need to have all of their needs provided by a government. Since everyone is powerless to create anything of value, social institutions must be set up to care for them. Any human enterprise that creates personal wealth or human value is evil and must be burdened with taxes to provide for those who lack courage or conviction to do the same. Life has no meaning and is painfully full of disillusionment; so, we can smoke cigarettes, drink poisons, take sedatives and pain killers, live dangerously, and otherwise attempt to destroy our long-suffering body. All of this goes back to our attempts to break away from millennia of mind control practiced in the form of religious and political tyranny.

Thanks to the North American experiment, political liberation has been possible and has spread throughout the world. So effective has this liberation been that European nations that have warred forever are now at peace with no thought of military conflict. Old feudal societies now practice democracy. The liberation of individual spiritual power is now under way as well, but it requires separation from the idea that some central authority must dictate to us what the world is about.

The self-reliance and independence that have been so critical to the formation of the United States need to be applied to spiritual matters as well. Once we are free of the chaotic control of a bewildering and ever-changing variety of official interpretations of what the founders of the world's great religions want us to do, then we can learn for ourselves what they intended. For example, when we expend less energy on whether baptism means sprinkling water over the head, immersion in a heated tub, or a trip to the river, we can spend more energy in exploring our own spiritual capabilities.

In addition to the teachings of all of the world religions there is another source of guidance that is now becoming known in the world again. This source of guidance has been known in the far-distant past but is now returning to us in order to provide us with powerful help.

We are never alone in our efforts to create our life. Each and every life is a collective enterprise. Just think of all of the people in your life, including the people you pass going in and out of the mall or stadium and those you pass on the highway. That is a frightening number! Now figure that each one of these people has half a dozen to a dozen guides around them helping them along the way. These same guides may not be with them through their entire life because guides are substituted in and out of service as they are needed in different stages of a person's life. In addition there are higher guides, angels and archangels, standing along the edges, to come in to help if needed. Even with all of this help, we still manage to get into trouble and to stray from our purpose. Our former family members or their spirit may also step forward from time to time to counsel us or nudge us in the right direction.

We are truly never alone. It is the height of foolishness to think that we are separate from heavenly guidance in the universe! Our guides try to keep us on course to live out the life plan that we laid out for ourselves. For instance, a person who, among many other things, was to come into this life to assist others with finances and who decides that she or he wants to be a teacher instead, will probably run into many problems in school. When we do what we set out to do, we generally prosper and succeed.

How do you get to know your guides better? There are many great books written about this, but the best way is to get quiet and begin to listen to the voices in your mind. To keep from heeding voices that will lead you into trouble, follow roughly the Ten Commandments. If you spend a lot of time and energy coveting someone else's possessions or donkeys, then these promptings and voices are not from your guides. You may discuss your desires and ambitions with your guides and ask for their help.

All of us are familiar with prayer. People all over the world pray in one way or another. Catholics are provided with a whole panoply of personalities to pray to. Hindus have this too. It is normal for people who think they need help to seek it from whatever they think is a source of power and strength. Who knows where these prayers really go. Our guides are with us from before we are born, so they know our situation well. They also know our character. It is as natural to request help from them as it is to ask it from any other divine source.

Again, it is necessary to spend a lot of time in quiet places and alone. Whether you spend this time in meditation or not is not important. Just listen to yourself. Become aware of the promptings of your heart and have the courage to try out some new things. We often hear nowadays about intention and manifestation of what we want. This is what our guides are for. They will definitely help us manifest what we need to live out our life plan or simply help us be who we are. Try to have the courage to respond to inner promptings to do something for ourselves instead of listening to all of the media clatter so present in our world.

Help from our guides places us in direct access to the infinite power of the universe. It provides us with a whole new outlook on what we are about in our earthly existence. We literally walk with divine guidance at every moment, and we cannot go wrong if we continually heed the subtle clues provided for us. We will look at every person that we meet and every event that we experience as a doorway to the divine. Everything that happens will say, "Opportunity, opportunity." Our guides will give us the power to step through doorways to new opportunity. They are waiting for us to acknowledge them.

The best way to begin is to declare our gratitude for the help that comes to us each moment. The more we feel grateful, the more there will be things to be grateful for. This begins the childlike sense of wonder so necessary to spiritual success in our lives and especially in our relations to each other. When opportunities arrive to be of help to others, even in a small or anonymous way, we must have the courage to act. Even a silent prayer on someone's behalf can help a lot. This helps us and gives us strength.

Our guides came forward at the moment that we decided to enact another life in the world. They know why we came into the world and what our life plan is. They know a lot about our other lives. That is why they are so useful to us. That is why we must understand that they are with us always and can be called upon to help us. No intermediary is required. No one is needed to intercede for us with our guides. They are like a family that is immortal.

When a deceased family member appears to us to warn us or encourage us, we should remember that in past or other lives that family member may have had a different role. Now we say, "My grandmother came to me in a dream last night." In another life your grandmother may have been your son or daughter or husband, etc. What is important is that this kindred spirit appeared to guide us. This shows that other souls who have been with us in many lives are keeping track of our progress and will step into our world briefly as the need arises. In the same way, the neighbor down the street that seems so familiar may have been a close relative in another life, even a brother, sister, mother, or father. So, we are not alone because those who helped us plan our life are along for the ride, so to speak. We are not alone because those who have lived other lives with us may appear in spirit form or may be part of our present life. This knowledge should be encouraging and comforting in difficult times. It should help us rethink how our life comes about. It should help us know how we are doing.

Of course, the next question could be, "Where is God in all this?" And then may come the objections, "Where are Jesus, Buddha, Mohammed, Zarathustra, or any number of other named prophets and teachers?" As for God, the overall impulse, motivation, inspiration, and ultimate guide for all this is what in modern Western Germanic languages is called God. In Western Latin-derived languages, it is called Dios, Dieu, Theos, etc. In Middle Eastern languages, the word is more like 'lah or 'wah, and in Far Eastern languages such as Chinese or Japanese, it is something like Shangdi or Shen. In the Orient, there is less of an idea of a single patriarchal God as in the West. This Oriental idea of spirit or divine power in all things is shared by people in Africa and in South America who are not Christian and by many other such native people, such as the Aborigines of Australia or Maori of New Zealand.

As for teachers and prophets of the last couple thousand years, besides the fact that they all taught pretty much the same basic moral ideas, however distorted these ideas may have become in the renderings of various religious causes, it must be kept in mind that their teachings are worthy of study and to be heeded.

Their inspiration was no doubt divine. We have really only fragments of their overall message, but these fragments have proven powerful enough to change civilizations. Of equally powerful messages from 10,000, 20,000, or 100,000 years ago, we know practically nothing. This is to say that divine revelation for guidance and moral rectitude is a continuous process that has been ongoing for many thousands of years in this world and in many others, but to fixate zealously on one single source of revelation from one fixed point in time is a very limiting method of spiritual education. Of course since these basic messages have so much in common and are endowed with such powerful ideas, any one will do as long as they are not clothed in the corrupt ambitions of people who see opportunities for profit and personal power. Here the chaff must be separated from the wheat.

We often hear nowadays, "You can if you think you can." This saying certainly characterizes the tremendous break from the past that has resulted in the United States and other successful democracies around the world. More breaks with the past following this saying can produce even greater results. Positive thinking can produce anything. Negative thinking only produces stagnation and stasis. What is needed is movement toward more spiritual freedom and personal power.

Chapter 3

What We Are

What follows are the "channeled" remarks of at least six or eight different non-earthly souls who have distinct identities, names, histories, etc. They each have a distinct appearance, and most importantly, they each have a distinct voice. Sometimes the narration is a composite of several voices; sometimes it is distinctly one single voice. In some cases, I am quite aware of which one of my guides is speaking at a certain time. I have chosen not to identify specifically which guides are narrating at any one place in the text. I feel that the ideas that are presented are much more important than a description of how such ideas might have come to me which would be distracting and deserves to be discussed in another place. The term non-earthly is not really fair because these guides are easily as involved with earthly life as we are. They certainly share our concerns for Earth life, and most of the time when they speak of our life, they say "we." There are many parts of Earth life that are important, but which are not perceptible such as gravity, solar energy, and radio waves. In the same way there are many spiritual forms of life on Earth that are not perceptible. Hence, when some of the discussion seems to be incredible, I can assure you that it seemed that way to me at first as well. I would literally run out of the room grumbling and muttering to myself. Sometimes it would take some time before I could integrate the new ideas into my everyday thinking, but that is the point of this whole book: to provide a way to understand our reality that has been largely lost to everyday Earth consciousness for thousands of years.

We need to rethink our ideas of who or what we really are. We began our life as a conscious being that was purely an idea of God. God wanted us to be, so we are. This conscious being has no form or shape. It is not composed of anything. It is just an idea, just energy. The form of this consciousness depends on in what realm it chooses to inhabit or manifest itself. All activity of this conscious being is for the purpose of becoming more like its Creator. Therefore it is natural that this being would want to create. In the Earth expression of this desire to create, consciousness, or our soul, projects out ideas in the form of energy. This energy forms tightly concentrated centers that appear as matter to our senses.

Our earthly consciousness is expressed as matter. We have senses to allow us to experience and participate in our earthly creation. These senses have a nonmaterial form and a material form which are the bodily senses. In other words, the soul, the eternal spiritual form of our conscious being, has the power to see, to hear, to touch, to taste, to smell. The same senses in the earthly body are approximate analogies of the senses of the soul. We know from near-death narratives, automatic writings, and other communications with those who are no longer in earthly life, that they commonly relate seeing relatives, great halls, and green pastures. They relate that they hear heavenly music that is not rock and roll, that they enjoy gardens full of heavenly fragrances, that they touch things that are soft, etc. They also relate that they feel joy, angst, excitement, and other emotions. From these reports, it is clear that there are senses that are not specific to the material earthly body. It has also been demonstrated that the extracorporeal mind has the ability to remember and reason. There are reports from those who are in heaven that they attend classes; that they have things explained to them; and that they clearly remember the events of their life on the Earth.

The point is to establish that the soul is a sentient, rational form of consciousness. As a sentient, rational form of consciousness, it is also very powerful. It can create everything that it needs to conduct its earthly life. It creates these things by projecting out energy according to a plan. These projections are also made in cooperation with other souls who are living with the soul in this life. There is an individual life plan and a collective life plan. There are individually created things and collectively created things.

Some examples of collectively created things would be neighborhoods, the weather, the sun and stars, and emotional atmospheres. Some examples of individually created things would be the body, personal possessions, the interior of a dwelling, and moods. The soul is very powerful. It is more powerful than anything in the earthly existence. It is more powerful than anything in the universe that is made of matter. This power has not been put to good use in the past. It has mostly been forgotten up to the present. People think that they have no power, no ability, while they are creating all that is about them all the time. People think that they are powerless, while they create the sun and moon in their daily life.

The "place" that the soul occupies during its earthly involvement is located between heaven and Earth. The soul may move between heaven and Earth as needed and whenever needed. From this place between heaven and Earth, the soul projects energy into the Earth world as it has been instructed and as it has agreed to do according to a certain plan. It cannot project just anything. Dinosaurs are no longer part of modern life. This projection continues until its life themes and purposes are fulfilled, and then it alters its projections to provide for the earthly experience of death. According to its plan and the consequences of its earthly actions and decisions, the soul may linger close to earthly life for a time in Earth terms. Then it continues with other activities and projects beyond Earth.

The soul is eternal. It does not perish. It does not cause anything that is not matter to perish. There is no cessation of being, only progress, however painful and slow. Communication with all souls is possible according to belief. You can if you think you can. As it says in the Bible, "As a man thinketh, so is he." Love allows all possibilities, all communications as is demonstrated here.

Among the many collectively created items of Earth existence are minerals, plants, and animals. It is mutually agreed upon among those who are participating in this Earth life now actively or out of material time latently and among those beings who supervise the conduct of earthly existence, which minerals, plants, and animals will be part of earthly existence in any one epoch. As was mentioned earlier, dinosaurs are no longer fashionable. Just as it is explained in the book of Genesis in the Bible, God gave humankind dominion over all of the animals of the Earth. So this is a long-known fact. It is a fact that simply has been forgotten, but not completely. During the late eighteenth and the nineteenth centuries, European writers and philosophers influenced in part by Eastern ideas discussed and debated the idea of the transmigration of the souls. According to this idea, mineral consciousness could progress to plant consciousness, plant to animal, and animal to man. Hence, writers encouraged everyone to pray for rocks, plants, and animals in order to speed along their progress toward human consciousness. Really there was no need for this except perhaps in a general way because all of this was already part of human consciousness. Minerals, plants, and animals are created by human consciousness according to what is needed at the time. That is why there are many life forms that no longer exist, because they are not part of the current program. For example, there are many species of apple that are no longer cultivated because species with different characteristics are needed now. In modern times the mineral uranium is much in demand as are tungsten and aluminum. In past centuries, copper was as prized as its cousin mineral gold. It is still highly prized, but tin, which was combined with copper to make bronze, is not as important as before. Today there is a periodic table of minerals to which additions are made as is needed. Five hundred or more years ago, most of the minerals on our periodic table were unknown. Even among animal species, discoveries are being made, and many species are threatened with extinction. The makeup of the natural world is obviously not exactly a fixed entity, but is flexible and subject to evolution and change. These changes are brought about according to changes in the themes and activities of human existence.

This modern age is all about removing the accumulations of erroneous thinking from the past that have limited our development. We can learn a lot from our modern devices. Our television, for instance, provides us with images projected on a flat screen that, by means of perspective geometry, the brain interprets as three dimensional or as having depth. We have no trouble with this whatsoever. It is now possible to dispense with the screen to some extent and project a hologram out into the air. We wonder at this, but accept it nevertheless. Now scientists and engineers have created the devices that do these things; so, how much of a jump in thinking does it have to be that we may do similar things with the reality that we create with our senses? On the one hand, each sense has its own reality; on the other hand, each type of reality has its own characteristics.

Our visual reality comes about in the same way as the television image or the image that a painter daubs on a canvas with color. Our soul emits the energy of the idea of a tree on the lawn before us and our eye creates the corresponding image for us including distance, depth, or dimension. What about color? Of course, as children we colored in the tree trunk as brown and the leaves as green. Our modern theories of light want it to be that the sun shines on the tree whose bark absorbs all color frequencies except brown, which is reflected back to the eye, which interprets the reflected electromagnetic frequency as brown. The same thing happens for the green leaves.

Still we are talking about the electromagnetic wave or signal reflecting from the tree to our eye. What if, in the same instant, we create the tree, the sunlight, the lawn, the eye, and the illusion of distance? We are perfectly happy when our television screen does this. Why can we not imagine that the same mental capacity that created the television image could also create the visual reality before us? Not long ago, there was no television in the world at all. Where did the idea come from in the first place? Could it be that the idea came from an awareness of how we create our visual reality?

We need to begin to think of the digital form of all that we perceive. Most of us vaguely know that a movie displayed on a screen from a TV signal or a DVD is originally composed of 0's and 1's; that is, binary codes. The images and print on a computer Website arrive in your computer in this binary code of digits. Your computer converts this digital signal, digitalized energy, into pictures and text. What forms of energy do we use to transmit our image of our body to those around us so that they may create it into matter that they can then see? When we look at our front, at our arms, legs, and belly, what forms do the signals have that then organize atoms into molecules, matter, and flesh and bone? What do the collective transmissions from all creatures associated with the Earth look like? What kind of energy waves are they so that when we receive them, we properly create grass, trees, stone, rock, dirt, etc.?

All of this gives the term *consciousness* new meaning. Consciousness breaks down etymologically into "to know with" or "to know" mutually, so, a rock or an iron bar or nail has consciousness however minimally in that their energy code is made available to our consciousness as part of its expression. If we want to experience an environment that features rocks, then we tune into rock frequencies, especially those appropriate for our geographical area. The rocks or rock ideas transmit to us what they look like currently, and we make them that way or project them. Thus the rocks, the trees, the land, our car, the Earth, the stars "talk" to us constantly so that we render them in ways that are useful to our life's purpose.

It is constantly noted that in the other world beyond our everyday living world—that is, the world of those who have passed out of this life, the world of our souls, and the world of the dead who are enjoying eternal life, etc.—there is no space and there is no time. We say technically that time and space are characteristics of the material world. Take away matter and there is no more time or space. We also happily say that our soul operates, exists in the world beyond time and space. Why can it not be, then, that the world that our soul creates for us to experience an earthly life includes the notions of time and space, of three dimensions and cycles of events that give the impression of time?

In science class, we were taught that matter by definition has weight and takes up space. No two chunks of matter can occupy the same space at the same time, etc. Matter experienced visually would not need these characteristics. It would only need to appear in our visual field. The sense of sight does not need weight or solidity. On the other hand, the sense of touch does need to feel solidity and weight. These sensations can be created along with the hand, the skin, and the tactile nerves in the same way that depth and dimension are created for the eye. These two senses can then be coordinated in the same way that we coordinate a bunch of dots on a television screen as a moving car that is about to crash into something and upset us. It all happens at once, and we experience it all with no thought otherwise.

In the same way, the necessary characteristics or sensations are provided for the senses of hearing, smell, and taste. All of these sensations are coordinated to provide an environment which is the instantaneous setting for that minute moral lesson in our life. When that minute lesson is over, the next setting is created and so on. But what about the sense that someone is in the room with you even though you have not seen them yet? What if you sense that they are standing behind you? What about the feeling that someone is going to call or that someone is in danger? What about the hunch that some action is going to come out one way or another or that someone is going to say or do something? We clearly have other ways to sense events in our reality that are beyond the five senses mentioned above.

You are visually and tactually aware of your front and your tactile senses confirm for you the presence of a back, but these are only the reports of your senses. We don't see our back most of the time because we are concerned with what is in front of us. This, too, is part of our creation, so that we live in a bubble that is our front and all that is before us including peripheral sensations. We constantly create this bubble received and confirmed by our senses. It is as if we pressed our face and our body into the membrane of a clear bubble and everything on the inside is our immediate reality. We then become part of the periphery of the bubble, but all that is necessary for us to live our life's purpose or theme is displayed in the interior of the bubble. This environment is altered at each instant as we move through our life plan. In this way, a certain rhythm is ongoing. We project, then participate; project, participate. This all happens with a rapidity which is beyond our senses, but everyone's universe is constantly following this rhythm of creation and renewal.

As is often mentioned in spiritual circles, you can sit in a quiet room isolated from noises and distractions and move your perceptual consciousness up and behind your head. From this point, you can see your body projecting its reality out in front of itself. Unfortunately, all around this image is profound darkness. It is possible to allow in images from other times, but this can cause a feeling of overwhelming confusion.

It is important to repeat what all spiritual guides and mediums remind us all of the time: we are never alone. We always have many guides and spiritual consultants, even angels at times, who help us each step of the way. So the dark envelope surrounding our image of our body with its reality projected out from it is only partially correct. This image may not include the many supporting entities that surround us at all times. With permission, however, these too can be viewed or brought into our awareness subtly. All we need to do is ask and be willing to accept without conditions whatever answers that we receive. There will be no negative or destructive answers.

If someone is with us, they transmit their image to us and we put them in our bubble. If it is a crowd, then we put the crowd in our bubble. Even in a crowd we can feel isolated or be aware of only a small area around us. Whatever we need at any time that we need it, we receive the information, the "data," to put what we need in our bubble. Anything may be in our bubble. We can take a picture of what is in our bubble. It is all there according to our beliefs, desires, and expectations, but it may be anything. If you want to change your life, you will be provided with the information and the necessary energy to do that. Some time may be necessary, but you can change.

What if we are at a basketball or football game or other sports event that involves multiple players all moving at the same time? Of course we have created cameras that can handle this. Why would it not be that we could receive and process the transmissions necessary to put all of this, the players, the crowd, the weather, and the airplanes towing banners in our reality bubble? If we are part of a television audience of millions for a sporting event, this is a collective experience, but for each of us, it is our particular life experience. What we watch in the televised event is the expression of the important principles of our life plan such as competition, striving for success or perfection, athleticism, camaraderie, team or group consciousness, national or regional striving or identity, and many other spiritual possibilities of which we know little or nothing. It is an event in which millions participate, but it is all us, each one of us.

Nevertheless, the eyes, ears, tactile nerves, olfactory nerves, and taste buds all participate in the creation of our living reality at each instant as well as other senses that we have not named or explored yet. When this life comes to its end and the corporeal versions of these senses are no longer needed, the soul continues on its merry way. It does not need to "go" anywhere, such as to heaven or to hell, or to rest, or to rise, or whatever. In other words, the soul is, so to speak, "in heaven" now and always has been. It always will be "in heaven." That realm, however roughly we understand it, is its natural state. When we "die," there is no need to go anywhere because "where" was an illusion created by the soul for our earthly experience. When that experience is over, so is "where."

Someone may object that we cannot possibly create a whole life. Every day we watch or read about whole lives in our various media. Of course, these can be so real that they leave us emotionally uplifted or drained. We create episodes of a whole life in our dreams, our imagination, and our memories that can bring about total emotional involvement, and which can have as much impact upon us as any experience in "physical" reality. Actually, not only can we create a whole life, but we can create one in which we are the principal character, the star. We have "written" our life story with heavenly guidance, and we are living it from moment to moment and from day to day.

The sensation of motion is itself an illusion. We create this sensation in front of our eyes or, if there is a wind around our body, by having our creation flow toward us, toward our sensing organs. It must be remembered that, in our imagination, we may go anywhere without there necessarily being sensation of motion. As those who have had near-death experiences report, in heaven if you think you want to be somewhere, you are there instantly. This is also true for earthly existence in some senses. For those who can manage out-of-body experiences, they know that not only can you "see" a different location, but that if you want you can decide to also be aware of tactile sensation such as warmth or cold or wind or even odors. This may take some practice, but it is possible. The point is that, in your consciousness, you can travel and experience other "places" without ever moving your body to those places.

The physical sensation of motion comes from a continuous change in the created environment so that it appears to flow toward your senses, toward you. When you reach your destination, you properly create the physical environment and the physical appearance of whoever is supposed to be there. Since the sensations produce the same results in our mind whether we actually move through space and time or not, it comes to the same thing. Since travel involves the experience of the passage of time marked by our progress through our created space with the accompanying changes of light and so forth as the day or night wears on and since time is an illusion so that everything doesn't simply happen at once, then displacement of the body from one place to another does not actually happen. It only needs to happen to the extent that our mind experiences it for whatever purposes it may have. The same trip is going to be different anyway for each person who experiences it and from instance to instance. The real hazard is, as everyone knows, with many repetitions, we are consciously aware of less and less of the actual program of the trip. We become mostly aware of its beginning and end, our goals. If we are enjoying public transportation, this is inconsequential, but if we are in the driver's seat, this numbing of the senses is of great consequence.

So now you may ask, "Well, this must mean that if I want to buy a new house, all I have to do is think about it in detail and it will appear for me wherever I want it." In your imagination, this is certainly true, but functionally it must be true also for all of those whose life may be attached to your house. There may be many of those including builders, realtors, and people in the neighborhood. The house must fit appropriately into their life as well. Here enter all of the rules of society that govern possession of property, social interaction, and the arrangement and identification of locations, such as along a road, in demarcated squares, in perhaps towers, etc. Here again we are all connected together. It is necessary for you and the realtor to travel around together and for you to have your behavior tested as you pass through all of these new locations, meet new people, share space with others, evaluate your needs and goals, try out your powers of realization, etc. Maybe whoever is selling or renting a house to you is someone from another life, and both of you have a chance to relive an experience together in a better way. It is the whole experience of buying the house that is the most important, not the actual house. And then, it is the whole moral adventure of house buying that really matters. Did you come through it all with a new idea of who you are? Do you have a new idea of who you want your neighbors to be? Did you offend everyone wherever you went? These questions are what life is really about.

Simply ask any group of people who embark on a shopping trip, sit down to eat together, set out on a round of golf, or go to a baseball game or a soccer game, or any other social activity. What they will remember the most is how it all felt, how the interaction among them went. The actual physical events are only important as they affect these emotions about the social activity. What finally matters is our emotional bonds that are exercised by whatever activity we undertake together. The things in that activity, such as where, when, what, place, time of day, weather, the specific activity, whether it be social, sport, and so on, are just the props for the drama in which human souls measure their character.

Chapter 4

How We Live

While we each individually create our own reality, our own life, we also participate with others in our time in the creation of our environment, our customs, and our culture. I live in the mountains, so those who live here with me and I create the mountains, lakes, and streams. The mountains are giant geological records. The rocks record literally, like pages of a book, eons of geology. I find all of this exciting. It is possible to step into the mountains and pick up rocks that were formed a long time ago. Of course, these rocks are now part of now. We have the far-distant past as part of the structure of the present. All of these mountains, rocks, streams, rivers, lakes, and oceans must be maintained.

As we move about in this reality, the images that we create are governed in our consciousness by the collective understanding of what this should look like. In other words, we project out from our brains scenery that is previously agreed upon telepathically, if you will, by all of those who live in, have lived in, will live in or, in any other way, have to do with our region.

You want to think that when you plan your life before you are born, with all of those who will be part of your life at various times, it is like going to the amusement park or county fair. This time you will ride the merry-go-round, the water ride, and the roller coaster. In the next life you will ride the merry-go-round again and go to the haunted house and the hall of mirrors. You do not imagine that you and all who are at the amusement park, in fact, create all of it. You all imagine it! In a less-daunting form of understanding, you all create the amusement park, according to certain preconceived ideas of what it should look like, ideas based upon what you all need it to look like to act out your life-play or to learn what you expect to learn. The word expect is laden with meaning here, because it literally means in its ancient form "to see out from." In other words, when we expect something, we see it out away from us. We project it in front of our senses so that we experience it.

All of this is a radical departure from the generally accepted ideas of what we do in life and what we expect, but we experience miracles all of the time and pay no attention to them. In the spring, the trees change from bare branches and twigs. Then, depending on where it is spring, overnight or in a short time, the branches have leaves. We watch this every year without any thought. Then we have a huge tree that was once a tiny nut or seed. How does this happen? Yesterday we had a dog; today we have a dog and puppies. Yesterday we had a family of two or three; now we have another. A few years ago your children were small; now they tower over you and are adults themselves. We regularly take all of this for granted, but this is how we live. These miracles are in fact the tools with which we conduct our life. We expect to meet a mate and we do. We expect to live somewhere and we do. So in reality we are doing all of these things. They are not just happening. Nothing happens that does not have a purpose. There are no random props on the stage of life.

It is possible to show many examples of how we do change our reality all of the time. Two people can be driving down a road together and one will say, "Did you see that giant hawk sitting on the fence post?" The other, however, may say, "No, I didn't." The hawk was in the reality of the one, but not the other. There is the famous example of witnesses at an accident where each has a different version of what happened from their perspective. Even more drastically, it is possible to change our reality by changing our attitudes. Anyone with any experience with twelve-step recovery programs knows that there is a big emphasis on counting your blessings and being grateful for everything in your life. One time when I was desperately trying to find an Al-anon meeting in the town where I lived, I was driving through heavy five o'clock traffic. I was so upset and discouraged, frightened even, that I could barely cope with the traffic, the sunlight, and my grief at the loss of a loved one to alcoholism. Suddenly, I remembered the admonition of the people at the Al-anon meetings—"Count your blessings and you will change your world!" I had a very negative attitude, and I lived in a generally discouraged frame of mind. I really didn't think that I had very much to be thankful for, but since I was desperate to get through the traffic to a meeting where someone could help me, I decided dejectedly to try it. I slowly began to list in my mind various things that I could be thankful for and, at a certain point, the busy, threatening world in my windshield changed into a friendly, warm summer evening. Everything seemed to slow down and cool down. I easily found the street where my meeting was to be. Remarkably, my world was never the same from then on. The miseries of living with an alcoholic were never quite so severe, and I was able to manage much better. That change in my attitude moved me into a new world where I remained!

In the same way, if two people are walking on the beach and one of them is grieving for a deceased loved one, the experience can be quite different for that person. The grieving person may only experience the beach in terms of the absence of their loved one and feel cold and buffeted by the breeze. Her or his companion may feel that the beach is pleasant and warm with a soothing breeze. Extreme joy or extreme terror can radically alter our experience of an environment. In fact, our emotions color and shape our experience of our world. We all have had times when we were very busy or intently involved in some event; and we have no recollection of what the weather was like, even whether it was hot or cold! This disregard for outside conditions can last for days. Was there any weather during this time? We have to rely on others for the answer.

Another example of our creative powers is how we might experience something like an airplane. An airplane is a complicated thing (we probably think it is more complicated than a cow), but it started with the idea of an airplane. Even though an airplane is made of materials such as metal and plastic, these are forms of matter, and matter is just confined energy. Therefore the idea had to be converted into the forms of confined energy that we understand as metal, plastic. So the idea of an airplane had to be expressed in such a way that others could participate in making it and enjoying it. A drawing had to be made of an airplane. Now that is rendered on a computer. In order for this drawing to occur either on paper or by computer, a great number of mathematical formulas become involved to describe curved and straight lines, their relationship to one another, etc. Then there is the mathematics of the physics of the airplane, what makes it fly through the air. Still, all of this is just an idea. Once the airplane builders have made their airplane, their idea and the mathematical rendering of their idea remain in the ether, in the collective consciousness of all of those who participate in the technology of airplanes.

Among those who participate, of course, would be the passengers of a commercial or private airplane. When these passengers then think about an airplane or see the airplane, they avail themselves of the idea of the airplane in the ether and project that out of their mind before them. Their eyes "see" what they create and they act accordingly. So are we all aeronautical engineers? Well, yes and no.

We did not conceive of the idea of an airplane. We did not design and test the idea to make it practical according to the laws of physics. All we need is the mathematical formula, the program we would say today, to recreate the airplane in our own terms, for our own purposes. What we actually create is colored and laden with our emotional baggage at the time: joy, sorrow, anxiety, etc. Hence, we each "see" the airplane in a different way at any given moment, but the basic airplane still comes from the original idea and the energy of that idea. Further, because of our interests and the orientation these interests give us, some of us will respond to the enormity of the airplane, some to its symbolism—is it a new beginning, an escape—some to the mechanical details and wonder of the machinery, still others to the shape and form. So for each observer, the same airplane is a little bit different, and each one will focus on different details. When asked to describe their airplane, different observers would relate entirely different details. Once again, our mind is performing what may seem like prodigious tasks without our even knowing it. Once again we are capable of tremendous creative acts, all the while thinking that we are lucky to just get up in the morning.

Now, no one needs to see the entire airplane in all of its complexity. Everyone has his or her own airplane. The mechanics have theirs according to their mechanical specialization; the pilots have theirs, which is mostly cockpit and instruments; the hostesses have theirs; the baggage handlers have theirs; and the passengers have theirs. Frequent flyers probably rarely even look at the outside of the airplane, especially if they go through a loading corridor to get on. They only really see the passenger compartment and the passengers. We only need to project out in front of our eyes and other senses that part of any structure that we have something directly to do with. How many people get on an airplane and think of the wiring diagram?

Recently we went to a hospital to visit a friend who was there. We had not gone to that hospital for many years. The hospital had probably doubled in size, and two multistory parking structures had been added on to the front in addition to the one that had been at the rear. Construction was ongoing upon our arrival. It was difficult to find a parking space and then find our way through the parking structures to the hospital annexes and on to the part of the hospital where we needed to go: the ICU. Did we need to have an idea of the entire complex of buildings? Probably very few of the hospital staff even had an idea of the entire complex, especially since it was being changed constantly as new parts were being added on. Again, our interests were how to enter the parking structure, how to find an elevator that would give access to hospital buildings, and how to find our way through these buildings to the ICU.

Of course, there were signs that indicated what direction we needed to go. Also various hospital staff stepped forward to direct us. At each stage our consciousness was occupied with parking structure floor, corridor, passageway, elevator, corridor, double door, and specialized unit. We did not, could not conceive of the entire set of old and new buildings. The hospital for us at that time was a relatively small number of passageways and corridors and the corner of the ICU where we spent the afternoon. We only had to create each of these structures as we encountered and passed through them. There would have to be telepathic guidance from those who "possessed" the building from the standpoint that it was their area of work and activity, and there were, of course, signs and indicators fortunately.

The materials with which a structure is built are only important to us if we need to interact with, build, or alter those materials. If we undertake to drill a hole in a wall, then we are interested in its structure and composition. At this point the energy of the material may communicate with us spiritually, but otherwise we only need to "see" a superficial rendering. In this, we are guided by those whose minds had to do with construction and with making a building work for their purposes. These ideas, as are all ideas, are eternally in the ether.

If we are traveling on the Earth, particularly by means of an automobile, truck, or train, as we move from one place to another, the ideas of what the area we are moving through looks like are transmitted to our minds so that they may be manifested by us in our experience. In order to understand this, it is important to remember that our entire life is planned out by us before we are born. This plan includes all of the possessions and accoutrements we need to carry out our life. If we are to experience the physical trauma of a fall from a ladder, then we need a ladder and a building against which to lean it. If we are to cope with some emotionally challenging news in the midst of another challenging event in our life, some means of communication for that news must be provided, such as a cell phone, television, etc. So all of the supposedly modern devices that we are recently enjoying in our lives were thought out and designed previous to our appearance in our life. There is much evidence, both physical and spiritual, that these devices are not so new and modern after all, so it is very possible that the idea of their design, etc., could be in the spiritual world of mind and soul.

In this we are all one. At some point in our life, we planned to be living in a particular dwelling in a particular community with certain possessions. We and others planned that, as part of our lives, we would construct or manufacture those things that are needed to make this age appear as it was decided on by consensus among the souls who would be involved or affected. All of this is thought out before anybody emerges as "born" on the scene. Not only does your brother or sister decide to be part of your life in this time frame, but they decide that they will always wear bright clothes of a certain type manufactured perhaps by others on the other side of the world. Together you may decide that they will present you with a special gift of some object or other at a certain moment in that life. All of these material objects such as the bright clothes and the gift are magically provided at the appropriate time. We take all of this for granted.

We needn't. Actually, it is not all as rigidly fixed as it might seem. An appropriate analogy might be to think that you wake up one morning on a lakeshore with the intention of going fishing at some location on some other part of the lake. This intention could be a very simplified example of a life's purpose, and the trip across the lake to the fishing destination, the life's "journey." Naturally you set out in your boat, your body, for the fishing spot you have in mind, but along the way all manner of things may occur. You may be joined by another fishing buddy in a boat out on the lake; you may stop to admire a flock of white egrets on a muddy shore; you may decide to fish somewhere else along the way; you may encounter another boater who is broken down and in distress in the water; a storm may chase you back to your starting point, or, for some reason, you may change your mind about your originally intended fishing spot. Hence, you may have an overall intention or plan, but many events can occur to alter your plan or challenge you to make all kinds of decisions, moral or otherwise. This is a very simplified analogy of a life that may involve many more complex layers of intention and meaning, but it conveys the general idea of possibilities and free will.

In any case, it all comes back to ideas and energy. Once the idea is formed in our mind consciously or unconsciously, energy is created that moves out into the universe as a certain frequency and wave pattern. This idea can then take many other forms in other worlds or universes. In our world, ideas can bring about emotional reactions and action and eventually forms of matter. If someone forms the idea of riding a bicycle, then there is someone who will want to provide a bicycle to ride. Others will want to make the materials for bicycles and other things. Others will want to bring the materials forth from raw materials. Others will want to make the surfaces on which it is possible to ride a bicycle and other conveyances. In our world, the creation of materials and the manufacturing is carried out all over the world. We are all in this together. We are all sharing and participating in each other's ideas and desires. It has always been this way. It is becoming more and more evident that movement about the Earth in one form or other has always gone on.

Before you ride your bicycle or fly in an airplane, you may have a dream in which you are doing those things. The dream could have been very real, including, in the case of the bicycle, the wind on your cheek, the physical exertion to climb a hill, etc. This you were experiencing in its idea form. If you fall off of the bicycle in the dream, your body could still experience the physical impact as you dream. Everything you experience in the material world can be experienced in the mind as a dream, daydream, or vision. Once the experience is rendered into physical form, the laws of the material world, the laws of physics, are applied to shape the experience for our purposes. Does the bicycle ride convey fear or joy? Were new muscles created and new lung capacity for our benefit? How does the bicycle experience mix in with everything else that is going on in our life? Was the bicycle borrowed from someone? Does it lead to an encounter with someone? It serves our purpose in some way, the same way that a plane ride would.

The dream, daydream, or visions are just experiments, suggestions of probabilities that may be carried out according to the various rules of the material world. They are a form of experience that may have an effect upon us, but they do not become part of our material life until we make them so. We bring them about in our material life according to our purposes. These purposes, which themselves are ideas, then have repercussions throughout the rest of the material world. Might someone else be motivated to ride in a plane or ride a bicycle? Might someone else be motivated to talk about the one who did these things? Someone else in the material world would find that created event to be useful in their life and want to "share" it. A dream or vision until it is shared in the material world will not necessarily have the same impact. Of course someone might be able to read your mind while you are dreaming, but that is an extremely rare possibility. When an object is created in the material world to serve some purpose, then the impulse of energy necessary to create that object is sent out into the three-dimensional world. This pulse of energy reverberates throughout the material world to the benefit of all who might be thinking of something similar, either simultaneously or at a later time. We are constantly influenced, even if only subtly, by the ideas and actions of others. Everyone involved with the creation of the object is impacted by the energy that is created by the idea of the object itself and by the energy created by the idea of the purpose of the object. If no need or desire is present in a culture, then there is an absence of energy. Thinking creatively creates energy for all!

Pickup trucks can be used to show how we make our material reality. Our material reality is the manifestation of our spiritual existence. Everything begins with a principle, an idea, or a concept. A principle can be described as an idea that manages what happens in our world and how we experience it. Some examples might be honor, freedom, and trust. A principle in the physical world might be weight, acceleration, expansion, solidity, density, or liquidity. A principle in the material world can be expressed mathematically. For instance, $E = mc^2$ describes one way to change energy to matter and vice versa. It states that when matter m is accelerated by spinning or other motion to a speed equal to the square of the speed of light, $c2$, it changes into energy. A certain amount of matter yields a certain amount of energy, etc. This formula also describes how matter can be created by slowing down light until it forms matter. Light is energy on the way to becoming matter.

In our modern times with algorithms for computer programs and engineering, we can understand how things can be described by a computer formula. Boyle's law, $pV = k$, describes how a gas increases in pressure when heated or confined in a smaller space. This principle helps power automobiles. In heaven, in the nonmaterial world, everything is idea or principle. There may be principles for things that we have never imagined such as the principle of an emotional reaction to music, color, or certain actions such as kindness.

Now back to the pickup trucks. I have been driving down the road, which is purely an illusion, when I found myself surrounded by the cab of a pickup that was different from the one I was in. In each case the one that I was in was getting rather long in the tooth, and I was thinking about getting a new one. Anyway, suddenly *flash* I was in some other truck. This has happened for three different pickups! I could describe that the visionary truck cab was a different color than the one I was in at the time, that it had a different feel to it, and that the light was different. Sometimes I would get this flash several times, so I suspected something was up.

In my second experience with this, I had not changed my truck because I could not afford a new one. One morning, I was eating in a fast-food restaurant, which happened to be located right next to a used-car dealer with which I had done business in the past. In fact, it was where I had purchased the truck that I was then driving. Normally I wouldn't have been in the restaurant at that time, because at that time of year I was usually in another state on vacation. A family health crisis had brought me home. While I was eating my lunch, a voice in my head said, "We have your truck over here." "Over here" I took to mean in the car lot next door. I finished my lunch and went next door to enjoy my new truck fever. While I had been driving around thinking about trading in my truck, I had been making a list of what options or features that I wanted the new truck to have. When I got to the car lot, I found a white pickup, which was the color I had envisioned, with an extended cab, which I wanted and with a trailer hitch, four-wheel drive, and the right price, about $10,000. I bought three trucks over a ten-year period, each for $10,000. The truck had some other features, such as window tinting and shades, which gave the interior the "look" and light treatment which I had seen in my flash visions. The interior was also the color that I had seen, which was gray. Later I was to learn that this model year was the one I had read about in a barbershop magazine somewhere as being the best brand for that year. The only problem was, how could I buy this truck? There had been rumors of a long overdue raise in the school district where I taught, so I checked with the school treasurer, got a new salary scale, and discovered that, indeed, I could buy a new truck! "My truck" was right there all right. After I made the trade and got rid of a truck that was costing me lots in repairs every week and threatening to cost even more, I pondered how this truck that I had recently seen myself in could have appeared like that. My wife and friends declared that I evidently had the ability to manifest pickup trucks. I was skeptical of all of this, but I was dead sure that something had happened.

A few years later while I was still trying to work out the metaphysics of the appearance of the white truck and was worrying about what was going to fall apart on it next, I had another flash of myself in still another pickup with still another look and feel. This time I boldly told my wife that I was going to get a new truck and that it was blue with a dark gray interior and a strange reddish tint in the windshield. The white truck had to go, I knew, but I had no idea where the new truck would come from.

I went to my used-car dealer and put in an order for a truck of a certain make and a certain year. He advised me that now another brand had the best truck in his opinion, which I trusted. A little while later, after I had heard nothing from my trusted used-car dealer, I decided to see what the local dealer in that brand might have. This was a bold move, because I wanted a recent model year, and ordinarily I could not afford anything that would be found on the lot of a new-car dealer. All of the talk of my being a pickup manifester had made me bolder. I arrived on the lot of the new-car dealer near dusk. I just went there on a whim. They showed me a few trucks that were not right, and then I screwed up my courage and asked what they had in a truck that was only two years old. It turns out that one had just arrived on the lot!

Sure enough it was blue. It had an extended cab with doors and the exact running boards that I had decided to put on my next truck. It had mechanical lumbar support where my previous truck had electric and had stopped working. This was very important for my back problems. It also had the bed cover that I had intended to get because I liked the one my neighbor had. (Later I found out that they were very expensive!) The bed liner was better than anything I knew about. It was four-wheel drive and had a towing hitch. The reddish tint to the windshield was lacking however.

Since my former pickup had a cap on the back, I was able to make a good trade and come up with a price that I could afford. There were no more $10,000 pickups, but I was teaching an extra course load, and this time I got paid for it. Since I had enjoyed the window tinting of my former truck, I sought out a place where I could have this applied to the windshield of my new one. Sure enough, as I was driving home into the low winter sun with my new tinting strip applied by the husband of a former student, I saw that reddish glow in the windshield. The look was complete. I didn't even have to have running boards put on or a bed cover. Moreover, the bed cover lock worked with the electronic key button, and I had a keyless entry which I knew nothing about, but which I appreciate more and more. How was this possible? Every item that I had listed in my head and told no one was installed on the truck already except for a strip of tinting. Later I met the previous owner of the truck and he said, "You bought my truck." His employer had bought him a truck, so he traded in this new one that I now owned for a car. I replied, "Thanks for fixing it up just the way I wanted it."

Now, I thought, this manifesting stuff had gotten serious. I had to figure out how it came about. Everything that happens in the material world has a spiritual version that was formed as an idea somewhat prior to it. This is simple. We think of a doghouse, and we go and build a doghouse. We may make a drawing that shows dimensions so that we may buy materials and estimate costs. We may consider this drawing as a type of mathematical formula for the doghouse. In the case of the truck, someone had originally ordered my pickup truck from a factory, or someone had specified that combination of features expecting that it would be marketable. As part of my life plan I was to have a pickup like this and obtained in this mysterious way so that I would freak out and write about it. Freaking out about truck manifesting was in my life plan. Hence, I had influenced the truck manufacture, and the man who had bought the truck before me had as well. Our thoughts influenced the ideas that went into the creation of that particular truck. The truck itself and all others were built by souls who were manifesting themselves as factory workers. Others, who manifested themselves in the world as auto industry delivery truck drivers, had brought the truck to my community in the mountains where other kind souls were fulfilling a life plan as car sales people. The first owner had bought it from them and knocked the price down for me, and then it was my turn to "own" it.

Each soul in turn helped me have this truck. This is wonderful. I didn't even know that I had asked for it. I was just thinking of it. Each of these souls in this chain of responsibility had a thought about some aspect of this truck. Each one experienced it in some way, as a part to be manufactured and installed, as a vehicle to be loaded and delivered, as an item in an inventory, and lastly as a vehicle to be used and enjoyed. Everyone along the way was united in this chain of being outside of time and space, and each soul or group of souls created my truck in their reality as it was useful for their experience. In this way, in a limited sense, dreams, desires for things, material achievements and, of course, spiritual achievements that benefit someone in material ways like a new hospital or a school or a factory, all help hundreds and thousands of anonymous souls in other lives experience what they require for their life plan. The truck began as an idea and was brought into reality at each step along the way but in each instance a slightly different reality. Each one of us created a slightly different version of the truck according to how it fit into our life plan. In this creation, we were all united. We all helped each other with their life.

The material world then responds to our needs and desires, but this response is conditioned by our beliefs. If we think that something might be useful or helpful to us, but that we don't deserve such a thing, then our material world will reflect this conflict. We might have a house, for instance, but it will be in a bad neighborhood or it will not have carpeting or need paint, etc. Then there is the danger that we may very well be able to realize our dreams, but we may not be able to see beyond the material realizations themselves; so we get caught up in the pursuit of one thing after another, never being satisfied. The pursuit becomes the purpose.

The material world and all other things should contribute to our spiritual progress. We must understand that spiritual learning and advancement is the ultimate goal of all of our life's projects.

Chapter 5

What Do I Do Now?

So, you may ask, what do I do now? Be aware at the outset that you are projecting a whole bundle of intention to be here, just to maintain your presence. Have you ever thought about how much energy and determination it takes to maintain your consciousness and apparent physical presence in this world? You, your soul, and the Holy Spirit definitely want you to be here, and they want for there to be a here for you to be in. How do you do all of this? You keep an extremely complicated body going, and at the same time you provide for the appropriate environment for the experience of that body. You provide for a body and for a world for that body to be alive in.

Is all of this automatic? How is it automatic? Who or what is doing it if it is automatic? If you are not doing all of this and it is all automatic, then you don't really exist anymore than a rock. But you can make changes. You can go this way rather than that, you can change the color of the room, you can buy a new car, etc. A rock cannot do that. So, you are the one who is making it happen because you want to make it happen. You project all of this intentionality, will, purpose, out into this world along with everyone else who lives in the world with you. You *want* to be here, so you are.

Why would you and all of those around you want to be here? What is your purpose in expending, projecting all of this energy to create this experience? There must be some payoff. Maybe you are here because you want to make all of this be better, to make the universe be a proper reflection of God's will. In that way you are, in fact, also a projection of God's will.

You are doing a lot here. You are busy. You have a family. You have friends. You have a job. Think about it! What are you going to do next to make the universe better for yourself and for everyone around you? You have some ideas. They are very simple ones. They can be realized in small, easy steps.

First, of course, you must not try to carry any "baggage" from when you were making things better "before." There is no "before," only now. All that you can create is your now, and you

40

can create all of that, but before is not available to be created any more. Drop it. Forget all that you created with others in the "before now." In the now that appears before you in space and time, you have a reality which is composed of the physical trappings, the material things that surround you including the weather. You have other people who are with you as family, neighbor, business associate, friend, acquaintance, etc. You have your busy-ness or occupation; that is, "what keeps you occupied" or some activity or interest that drives you through each day. The word *day* is rooted in an ancient word for light, so the light is created each day to mark the time during which one is occupied with carrying out one's mission or purpose in this life. Some people do all of this in the dark, but for that they create artificial or unofficial light. When you are not active in the day, if it is night and you are asleep, you are really away working on other things and the body is put on the shelf, so to speak. The body is put to rest. It is parked while the soul is busy elsewhere. The soul does not sleep. When it is time to create another day, the body is roused; it continues to serve as the instrument through which this life is experienced.

The other people who are participating in this life with you, with whom you are sharing this experience, signal their appearance telepathically to you; you create their image for your eyes to see, if you are not blind, and you greet them in your daylight. Really everyone knows all of this; but in order to carry on through their day, their life, this knowledge, this awareness is put aside, because it can be distracting. Knowledge of all of this can also take away from the investment of energy needed to do all that is necessary to properly conduct one's life. A mechanic cannot both work on a car, tinker with its construction, and drive it in a race to win. The makeup of the car has to be accepted as a given once the race has begun.

At the same time, what you create is in fact an extension of your consciousness. There is no separation between you experiencing and what you are experiencing. The great scenery or the city or the Grand Canyon, that is before you now, is the extension of your consciousness. You had programmed your existence to experience this sight at this time and so you project it out in front of you. Do we marvel any more that a computer can show a viewer any side of an object that is asked for or any wall of the inside of a structure or body? These computers were created by human intelligence, so why should it be so hard for human intelligence to create a plausible working image of the Grand Canyon before its senses?

As it was required you transformed your body from one small cell into the magnificent creation that it is now. How much do you now resemble the plump baby you once were or the small child or the gangly teenager? Just imagine young women preparing for a body that will create new humans! Yet this is happening all of the time. It is time to be aware that you can do this, that you have done this, and that you will continue to do it.

As you are creating all of this, you are also creating time. Earth consciousness is experienced in linear dimensions, seemingly causal, with this event leading to that one. This is all illusory, but it is the nature of the experience. It therefore appears that one thing seems to happen before another; but when you dream about your life, the future tumbles out as if it were present. As anyone who has dealt with déjà vu knows, you often can recall when in the past you had the dream or vision of what now occurs in your present. The memory and the sensory event, the experience, are all now part of the present. Other aspects of your experience follow the laws of physics. In Aristotelian phenomenology, physics described the world experienced through the senses, and metaphysics explained the idea behind that world. Plato proposed the idea that everything appeared to our senses according to a heavenly ideal model. They had all of this discussion thousands of years ago, yet we do not marvel that this was known? According to the laws of physics for our time, as matter is created by the consciousness, it must behave in a certain way. It is like a complex chess game, but instead of chess pieces, you have types of matter. There are laws of relative impenetrability, or relative density, so everything may intermingle with what is classified as gas, but gas can only penetrate liquid if it is pressurized or animated by heat. Solids can penetrate liquids, and among solids there are ranges of solidity, according to molecular bond strength, so that sharpened metal may penetrate wood, but not vice versa. An extremely accelerated softer object may, however, penetrate a harder one, because of its greater energy. These are the laws of physics by which we organize the physical expression of our life. In dreams, these laws do not apply because dreams are pure idea with no energy expression in molecular form. These laws may not apply to imagination either. Whatever is created in molecular or material form is only fleeting because created space is constantly pulsating and being recreated below the experienced level of our consciousness. The application of energy to all of the molecular creations, which are only tightly wound bundles of energy, changes the nature of matter and the laws of density or interpenetrability. Hence hot iron becomes liquid, liquids change to gas, etc. Even solid matter is only relatively solid according to what is around it or its state of excitation due to heat or other forms of energy. Whatever form matter may have, it is because that is what serves our moral purpose at the time. We need matter in order to create the setting for our moral dilemmas that force us to make choices. These are the choices that teach us what it is to be like God.

The Rocky Mountains, the starry sky, or a great steel ship are created for you by your consciousness according to telepathic programs passed to each of us through the ether. The ether is very busy! If you are standing on a dock before a great cruise ship, how do you even know what it is if you have never seen it or experienced it before? Earlier you may have imagined standing there with a ship before you, but now you say that it is greater than you imagined. For weeks before your cruise, you dreamed and daydreamed about the experiences that you probably would have on the cruise. How did you do that unless you had some idea, some ideational resource as described by Plato, to help you make an image of a great cruise ship in your mind? In this way a tiny, elderly lady from Kansas can stand before the hull of a great ship and not think that the horizon had turned into a brightly painted steel wall.

There are all of these books published about the afterlife, about messages from "the other side," about what it is like there. Of course, there is no afterlife or before life. We don't go anywhere when we dispense with our interest in this life. We have these concerns because of fears engendered by the professional religious establishment. So-called spiritual knowledge has been taken over by the religious professionals as their exclusive domain. This happened a long time ago. Priests, ministers, pastors, and tyrants have reaped much profit from these fears. Anyone who showed any knowledge of the spiritual realm or who offered opinions that were not in accord with the established orthodoxy were labeled witches or heretics and eliminated from public access. We now enjoy books by people with various psychic skills who reassure us that everything is all right, and that those who have passed on are fine; that they are happy in a wonderful place full of beauty, music, and love; and, especially, that they did not go to that other hellish place. I have never heard of a medium reporting messages from a relative that said, "I am in hell."

We need these reassurances because of a basic misunderstanding. When we realize that the life that we are now living is one with our eternal consciousness, then there is no need to be afraid of an afterlife. There is not really an after and we do not go anywhere when we are finished with this life. Where do we go when we lose consciousness of this life when we sleep?

The best way to understand this is to think of our body as the puppet of our eternal consciousness. Our consciousness manipulates the puppet according to its role in the play, and the puppet certainly appears to have life. When our consciousness is finished with the play, it does not cease to exist, and it does not go anywhere. It just puts down the puppet and perhaps picks up another one. In reality, it is manipulating a myriad of puppets. To this analogy must be added the state of mind of an actor on a stage. Anyone who has ever acted, including in childhood games, knows that in order to play the part, the actor must be focused on the role. This focus may require considerable study to understand how one's character is supposed to act. In other languages, the actor or actress is said to *create* a role or *create* a character in a play, film, performance, or whatever. The actor has consciousness; he or she knows that it is only a play, a representation, but within the confines of the plot, the story, a good actor will appear to be the character he or she is assigned to portray; sometimes even considerably altering their appearance. When the performance is over, the actors do not go anywhere. They shed their identity as the character in the play and step to the front of the stage to take a bow. Our eternal consciousness does the same. Each time we sleep and when we are dead, our consciousness goes off to other tasks.

It is useful to combine the two metaphors of puppet and actor so that we will have a sort of conscious puppet that is manipulated electronically, wirelessly, in an elaborate setting of its own making for the purpose of experiencing some spiritual moral task. Now the "of its own making" part may not be as difficult to accept if we return to our childhood games of "let's pretend." When we were children, and we allowed our imagination more free reign of our consciousness, we could very well alter our reality so that a blanket thrown over a table was a cave or a spaceship or whatever we wanted. Anything could be anything, and within the rules of whatever we were pretending, all other reality would be temporarily canceled, denied. I have always been fascinated by how easily and with what intensity children fall into these games. Sometimes, if you are present in the middle of their games, you may just disappear or be assigned the role of a tree or other object. I have also been fascinated by the fact that children play this game at all.

With these analogies in mind, it is possible to see that consciousness, in the form of the overreaching soul, in the form of our living persona, in the form of a dream persona, or in whatever form, is all one continuous life. Even in this life, we occupy radically different forms. We begin as a single cell, then a group of cells, then a more organized group of cells, then as a dependent infant with no language and no control over our bowels and no ability to feed ourselves. Then we are a small child with limited abilities, then an older child, then an adult. Even as an adult, we change our form radically, by perhaps gaining or losing weight for example or by allowing ourselves to age according to preconceived notions. Do we say that the baby or child has died? Has the infantile body been abandoned? Where did it go? How different is it that, when it is all over, and we no longer respond to others, our body turns into a mass of minerals? We, however, are occupied with other things just as we always have been.

When we are creating our life, just as when we are acting in a play or pretending as a child, others are creating and pretending with us. We are constantly communicating with them, as children do, to regulate the appearance of the reality experienced, and all of this creating makes an experience from one moment to the next. However, it is perfectly clear to anyone that someone who is acting a part in a representation, a play, must be focused on that part. An actor on a stage could not act a part and at the same time carry on an argument with his mother-in-law. It just wouldn't work. The spell would be broken.

We do, however, move from one form of consciousness to another, such as when we sleep, meditate, or daydream. In such states we may lose track of time and of where we are or what is going on about us. How many people, for instance, have been on a solitary journey in a car or other conveyance and have become lost in thought only to find that they had traveled a considerable distance unconsciously. There is one fairly formal rule about consciousness and that is when we visit the realms where the material rules no longer pertain, we generally forget what we experienced or learned there. People who have near-death experiences often report that, after their encounters and experiences with beings on the other side, they are advised that they do have some life purpose to fulfill and that they will not remember much of what they saw and heard while on the other side. Many of the things that we may experience in our purely spiritual state are incomprehensible in our limited rational earthly thinking. How could Pinocchio, the puppet, understand, for instance, his puppeteer swimming in the ocean? So while we are performing our role in this life, we have little room in our earthly consciousness for forays into other forms of consciousness. We have to maintain our focus, or everything will get blurry and we will miss our cues. When we give up this focus, it is possible to be anywhere and do anything.

This is when people have intuition, inspiration, out-of-body experiences or do remote healing or viewing. When we shift our focus slightly, we may recall past lives or receive information intuitively. Hence we do not really stray far from our spiritual intelligence. Even in this life, we have transparent barriers, such as those in ball games, or social barriers, or political boundaries. There is no concrete wall at these barriers, but still everyone knows where they are. It is not such a stretch of the imagination to think that we are aware of the invisible barrier between the material world and the purely spiritual world. It is just that for the average person without proper credentials, say of spiritual adviser, priest, minister, or psychic, this knowledge is taboo. The average person is not expected to explore these boundaries. But why not? They have the same intelligence and abilities as anyone with the "necessary credentials." Once the idea that this knowledge is sacred, special, taboo, or reserved only for certain people is canceled, then anyone may traverse these boundaries to find what may be there. According to the beliefs of a culture or individual, a person who can tell fortunes, see through walls, or predict disaster may be looked upon as either good or evil.

Nowadays there are many books and other media with information on how properly and successfully to go about crossing the boundaries between our physical and our spiritual worlds. Jesus said in the New Testament, "Ask and you shall receive. Knock and it shall be opened unto you." He did not say for you to go and get a priest and have him knock for you. Nor did he say only a priest can ask or explain what God tells you. No credentialed intermediary is mentioned! If Jesus and the universe did not think that this was something for everyone, it would not have been offered. Jesus also taught that there are many "mansions" in his father's kingdom, meaning many realms of knowledge, consciousness, and many other things. This again would not have been mentioned were it not available to all. He said warmly, "I go there to prepare a place for you." He did not say, "Go get a priest to conduct you there." When you think of the teachings of all the other sources of spiritual knowledge, whose teachings have started great religions, why would they have explained and preached and suffered if they did not intend for everyone to hear and learn. Did any one of them hold seminars for a select few priests or specially appointed followers? Their teachings were for everybody regardless of culture or language. These teachings were taken over by a select few because there was power and profit to be had. All of these attempts to control these messages have now failed, and everyone can study and evaluate them on their own. And everyone can use these teachings as launching pads for more knowledge. The doors of all the sacred temples are now open. Search therein!

Chapter 6

What Do Our Senses Really Tell Us?

Our biggest problem with accepting that we are creating all that is happening around us is in what we understand by out there or here. In other words, if we object to the idea that we are creating everything around us, it is primarily because we sense that what is around us is different, differentiated from our bodies and our sense of consciousness. If we are standing next to a building, obviously the walls of the building do not look like flesh and bone; they do not look like skin. It would certainly be creepy if they did. We are standing on the Earth, and it appears to be solid. We do not sink into it. The air appears quite different from our body in that it is transparent. We are only aware of it as it somehow brushes our skin. All of these sensations that make other things distinctly not us are received from our sense organs. However, our sense organs are not quite what they seem.

The five physical senses are not necessarily rooted in the physical body. Plenty has been said about the unreliability and the deceptions to which the physical senses can be subject, but nothing much has been noted about the more obvious functioning of the analogous versions of the physical senses independently of the body itself. The first examples that come to mind are those of reports of near-death experiences. People who have been pronounced clinically dead in hospital settings, for example, have reported later that they saw their body lying on a bed or operating table, that they saw medical personnel struggling to revive them, etc. Sometimes these experiences occur at the scene of accidents as well. In any case, those who were injured or ill to the extent that they were apparently dead, later describe having seen their body in a state of distress in a dramatic environment. Sometimes they also report hearing conversations among rescuers or caregivers and experiencing other sensations.

Often the narrator of such an experience reports looking down on the scene in which their afflicted body is found so that their perspective, or literally the position of their eyes, is above the actual scene. It is understood that the part of the person that is seeing, observing, witnessing, and mentally recording this experience has risen up out of the body. What is mostly never mentioned is some question as to how the narrator can see their invalid body when their eyes are in that body, are closed, or are attached to an unconscious mind. In other words, in these cases, the sensing organs, the eyes, are not functioning, yet the patient who relates their experiences after the fact—and there are many such stories—nevertheless sees and remembers what was happening.

Now, many mental processes are needed in order for this witness to such an experience to occur. First, of course, there must be eyes to see. Then, there must be memory in order to understand what is occurring and place it in the proper context. In other words, in the case of a patient who dies in a hospital room, the disembodied witness must have the same memory as the dead patient. They must understand that indeed this is their body on a bed in a hospital room with appropriately attired medical personnel in attendance and that these personnel are trying to revive them instead of trying to harm them, bring about their birth, send them to their death, or just anything else. So there must be a reasoning mind with a memory behind the functioning set of eyes. Just imagine bringing a Stone Age jungle dweller onto the same scene and asking them to explain what is going on here. Or if the witness were some visitor from some other time, some ancient or future civilization, would that witness interpret the scene in the correct way? A narrator that reports hearing the comments and exhortations of people in such a scene would also have to know the language of the people and why they were saying what they were saying. Without a proper context, words and sentences have little or no meaning.

Lastly, the witness would have to have the rational capacity to evaluate the scene, to understand expressions of urgency or alarm, and to be able to predict and evaluate the probable outcomes of the activity in the scene. Now these are all rational, sentient processes that should be found in some part of the brain matter of the unconscious or deceased body being observed; yet they are functioning normally without the brain cells. Is it therefore possible that vision, memory, and reasoning ability are not specific to brain cells? It appears from all of this that, in fact, the workings of the mind and the mind itself are extracorporeal. Curiously in the French language, for one, the word for mind is spirit, *esprit*. In other words reasoning, reception, and evaluation of sense data and memory are part of the soul. The body is only a participant in all of this.

Other examples can be given where there is the experience of sensation without any source in the physical world. Many people who have lost beloved pets can relate experiences of hearing a dog's toenails on the floor, a collar shaking, and a dog lapping water out of a dish that is no longer in the place where the sound used to come from. How does this occur? There is no sound in the physical world and nothing visible to make the sound, but still multiple people can report hearing it. Of course there is also the often-reported sensation of smelling an odor or pleasant fragrance from a long time ago that seems to be prompted by some event in the present or a recollected memory of an event. Here, the source of the sensation is no longer present, but seems to be recalled from the memory. The same thing can happen in the case of a memory of how something felt, such as someone's touch or the surface of an object. The sense of taste can also respond to memories, so that a distinct taste can recur on the tongue when the source of the sensation is long gone.

People who tell of the experience of sensing ghosts, and there are many such tales, often have multiple sensory experiences. They may report having seen something; others present at the same incident may not report seeing anything but will report hearing or smelling something. Some may report a sensation of coolness or get a chill where others feel warmth. Once again, sensation is present, but there is nothing in the physical world to bring it about.

To return to the near-death experiences, those who can report such an experience often speak of somehow passing through a tunnel at the other end of which they recognize the forms and faces of other people who have died previously. Again this requires a visual recognition, a memory, and rational understanding in order to put all of this information in a context.

All of these are examples of sensation absent either a sensing organ or a typical source for sensation in the physical world. These are also examples of cases where there is either memory and reasoning without brain matter present or sensation brought about by memory instead of physical stimuli. In any case, sensation can occur without the presence of the sensing organ: eye, ear, nose, tongue, fingertip, skin, etc., or without the presence of the expected source of sensation: light, something to make a sound, some vapor to smell, something to touch. The mind is able to process any form of these sensations regardless of the presence of brain cells or the presence of physical stimuli.

One extreme form of the last conclusion is remote viewing. The sources of images in the mind are far from the physical body of the viewer. Clearly the eyes of the viewer do not leave the body, but the mind/brain can certainly evaluate the viewed scene. Street signs can be read, traffic patterns can be understood, and the nature of a scene can be interpreted usually: city, country, port, water, hall, etc. This is not always the case, so the sense of sight brings in information that the mind and memory are incapable of interpreting, and it requires the knowledge and memory of another person to interpret the information. An even more extreme version of such seeing, or visions, is that of hypnotic regression, where a person is led by hypnosis to report what they see in a past life. Here, there is recourse to experts and extensive research to interpret what is reported and even this is to no avail at times. In this case, the sensation of sight, absent the use of the eyes, is bringing in information that the mind of the seer is unable to process. The sensation of sight present only in the mind goes beyond the brain's intellectual capacity for evaluation and interpretation. In these cases, it may take some time and the discovery of previously unknown information before what has been reported by the vision of a person subject to hypnotic regression can be understood. Hence, vision without the use of the physical eyes can provide information that the mind can report, but cannot understand.

It is impossible to discuss such experiences without bringing up dreams. In dreams, things are seen, heard, smelled, felt, tasted, and experienced even though the organs usually assigned to these sensations are turned off. A dream sound may startle. A sound in the environment of the dreamer may be incorporated into a dream. It is accepted that the mind of the dreamer is not totally shut down because various brain wave probes have revealed different states of consciousness or unconsciousness during dreaming such as REM sleep and others. Where the sensation of sound, sight, etc., comes from during sleep has not been found, however. Nor has it been explored how a dream may seem so real to the dreamer that arms and legs are moved, shouting occurs, sweating occurs, and other bodily involvement occurs. Apparently the brain is unable to distinguish between sensations brought about by stimuli from extracorporeal sources and sensations whose sources seem to be from within the brain itself. The brain's inability to make this distinction naturally begs the question of just what a sensation is. Some sensations, as well as emotions, may be brought about by electrical probes in the brain. I used to be able to cause a certain smell in my nose by touching my elbow in a certain way. All of this adds up to the necessary conclusion that the experience of sensation may occur from various means, among which are the organs of sensation located on the body. If these organs do not exclusively produce the sensations by which we experience our life, by which we conduct our life, then what do they do?

Our five primary sense organs—eyes; ears; tactile nerves including heat, cold, texture, moisture, etc.; taste buds; nose—are responsible for reassuring us of the proper composition of our reality. In other words, they tell us how we are doing. If it is December, and the ground is covered with snow, it is unreasonable to create a day where the sun is blazing hot at 100 degrees Fahrenheit. If an automobile passes by and sounds its horn, that sound should occur within a certain decibel range; otherwise, there is something amiss. What is supposed to be rough should feel rough; what is supposed to be smooth, smooth. These things are, however, relative depending upon our emotional state. To someone with a burn, what may seem smooth may feel rough. If someone has a fever or is in an extreme emotional state, a warm December day may feel much warmer or much colder. Our senses confirm the projection of reality that we need in order to experience our life. For some who believe this projection is all there is, that this is the extent of reality, then these confirmations are taken at face value for reality. For others, who know that there is another spiritual reality that is not material, then these confirmations are taken as approximations.

There are other more abstract factors that may also control our perceptions and what our senses "tell" us. These factors control not only what we experience, but also our interpretation or evaluation of it. A good example is Santa Claus. If a child is older and has been properly indoctrinated with the idea of the beneficence of Santa Claus and how he sees all childhood conduct and registers approval or disapproval, then that child, when placed in the red lap of Santa Claus, may smile, coo, and speak warmly to the Santa Claus impersonator. If, however, a child is younger and cannot really understand the indoctrination as to who or what Santa Claus is, then that child will burst out crying and shed tears and fearfully push away the Santa Claus impersonator. What is more interesting is that Santa Claus only exists in the minds of people who are part of Western culture or those who choose to imitate Western culture. Santa Claus has had many versions over the past five hundred years or so, and the one we most see now was created by a soft drink company!

But wait! There's more! The actual word Santa Claus in the English language, which is the widely recognized term, is a fake word that has evolved from a Dutch mispronunciation of a French word. Saint Nicholas changed to Sint Niclaus, then to Santa Claus, all the while moving from the forests of Alsace-Loraine in France to Holland and then to the USA. So Santa Claus is a belief shared by a specific culture for the purpose of pleasing children and livening up the darkest days of a northern winter. This is purely belief based upon some vague event in the distant past, and which carries a name vaguely reminiscent of the past event. Some see all of this favorably and embrace it wholeheartedly; others do not. We have many such beliefs that are part of our national culture, our regional culture, our family culture, and our personal outlook on life. There are some people who will step forward and say that the cells in our body harbor beliefs brought forward from genetic memories! All of these beliefs affect, even control, what we allow in our life as our reality. If we think Santa Claus is ridiculous or worse, repugnant, he will more than likely not appear in our world. If we think he is wonderful, he will appear abundantly.

To extend the argument to another example, if we think women are inferior to men, then everything that we perceive about women will be affected by that belief including whether we ignore women totally and do not even see them. On the other hand, if we believe that men and women are in all ways equal, then we enjoy a totally different world. It is possible to see the reality created by these two opposite beliefs in our world. In societies where the sexes are not treated equally, this belief controls how houses are built, how business is conducted, how education is provided for, and how economic progress is maintained. Clearly from a very general point of view, a society that practically denies the existence of roughly one-half of its population is going to be handicapped.

On a purely individual level, what if a person were to harbor the belief that money is evil and that it is morally wrong to seek or receive wealth. It is reasonable to expect that such a person would not enjoy much prosperity and would not profit from opportunities for personal gain, etc. Such a belief can be part of a family culture for generations. It can be part of a neighborhood culture. It can be used to justify resorting to theft or narcotic blurring of reality such as legal or illegal drug abuse.

Beliefs can be subtle, buried beneath the surface of our consciousness, and difficult to root out. The belief that even secret family behavior such as substance abuse, incest, physical abuse, and other mental illness is cause for a feeling of shame on the part of members of that family when in public can be so far below the surface that a person will never be aware of it. Beliefs sometimes work in tandem. Someone might believe that wealth is evil, but that it is important to put up a good front and impress your neighbors and friends. Beliefs can be in packages. For instance, the belief in the inequality of the sexes is usually part of a group of beliefs that result in the oppression and restriction of large segments of a society and of strangers. The set of beliefs that allowed the enslavement of Africans also resulted in bringing out monstrous behavior in their "owners." These are examples of the negative results of beliefs with which everyone is familiar. They are important to show that obstacles to the prosperity and happiness of individuals within a culture can lie in the beliefs held by the members of the culture.

Beliefs, of course, can have a totally different result. We often hear, "You can if you think you can," or "I believe in miracles." Tommy Lee Jones is credited with saying, "I believe in staying positive. It creates opportunities." Norman Vincent Peale made a career out of encouraging people to be positive about their beliefs. He filled his wonderful books with examples of how beneficial results were obtained by people who switched from negative to positive beliefs. Many times when a group or an individual sets goals for themselves, all sorts of opportunities and people will appear from seemingly nowhere to help them. What is important here is that these examples point to the possibility of creating helpful, beneficial situations in reality where none seemed to exist before. Quite literally we are often taught, as in the Tommy Lee Jones statement, that beliefs create new reality.

We all are literally composed of bundles of beliefs. They influence the very appearance of our bodies. They influence what our living space looks like. They create opportunities and encounters. They invite people into our lives. They structure our lives. Beliefs are extremely malleable. If you discover that you have a belief that is making you ill, hurt, miss promotions, or live in poverty, you can change it. Very soon you will see new things in your life. You will have created them by altering your beliefs. Requesting divine or spiritual assistance in this endeavor is helpful, but you must be ready to accept and exploit to the fullest the changes that come about.

What about those people who live in a negative repressive environment? How can new beliefs change their life? Everyone has his or her own specific experience of those circumstances. In the case of a thunderstorm, for example, some may be struck by lightning, others not. Some thought the storm was frightening, others that it was beautiful. In the world of sports, you can have an athlete who plays for a losing team in a losing season, but who has excellent personal statistics and moves on. I have given an example elsewhere where I changed my whole world by changing my attitude. The people didn't change. The negative behavior of others kept on going, but I became interested in other things. The secret there was to develop the positive attitude that I lived in a world full of things to be grateful for. You need only to create your own life and the world where you live that life. You can create it. You are creating it. Examine your beliefs, keep an open mind, accept your strange ideas that you didn't know you had, and fix them. Don't let anyone else interfere. Don't let anyone else hold you back because you no longer share their beliefs.

So what our senses tell us depends on our particular focus in any given moment, on our emotional state, and on our beliefs. The reality in which we operate is not absolute. Regardless of the numerical temperature, some people may say that it is hot and some people may say that it is cool. We may each have a completely different reality. Some of us may have things in our reality that are completely absent in the reality of others. A good day for golf may not be the best day to fish. The information that our senses give us with which we experience our reality, our life at any given moment, depends on our individual needs in that moment. We filter, color, and influence our sensory experience according to our life's purpose at any instant.

As we all know, our senses can play tricks on us. They may even gang up on us and give us a shock. This is what happens when our senses report a déjà vu experience.

Chapter 7

What Can We Learn from Déjà Vu?

Déjà Vu—My Experience

My earliest memories of déjà vu experiences are not so much of any particular incidents, but more of the shock and fear that the experiences caused in me. Because I moved around a lot as a child, it was possible for a great variety of déjà vu experiences to occur, experiences of radically different settings in different countries with different cultures, completely different school settings, etc. This made the experiences distinctly unique and unmistakable and all the more shocking. Anyone with experience with déjà vu knows that when the perceptions appear, they can be stunning, physically stunning. They can be like a blow to the chest, and they can knock the breath out of you. All of this can be very frightening for a child. Naturally I didn't mention the events to anyone or attempt to discuss them. Really I didn't know how. I may have assumed that these things happened to everyone, which apparently they do.

I do remember that as a teenager, I decided that one way to deal with the abrupt shock of the experiences was to begin to analyze and study them. In a few years, I came to the conclusion that they seemed to occur at times of big changes in my life; for instance, after a move to another country, another environment. They did not necessarily happen just before or after some big event such as an injury, a death in the family, or a trip. Déjà vu, at first, was not ominous. It did not seem to foretell some great stressful occurrence in my life, but instead seemed to tell me, "You are on the right track. You are where you are supposed to be. This was meant to happen." I remember reading somewhere in a very rare discussion of déjà vu by a Canadian woman that she was looking out the window of a moving railroad car and realized that indeed she had seen it in a vision before. She went on to reflect in her article that she had had no such visions telling her of the imminent death of her husband, the loss of her house, or other such life challenges. In other words, the déjà vu moment was extremely innocuous, revealing no great life event or change. It only seemed to say, "This is where you were meant to end up when it was all over."

One aspect about déjà vu for me was that I was able to recall fairly well at what moment I had actually seen the vision or scene that was shocking me into recollection. I could say that I had seen the stunning setting now before my eyes some three, four, or ten years previously when I was living in completely different circumstances. So, to simplify, when I lived in small towns or cities, I would have visions of mountains and country-side. When I lived in the middle of the country, I would see the ocean. Or when living in one house with a certain group of people, I would see another house with a different group.

At one time, I launched into a fierce and frightening analysis of how I could see things ten or more years ago that would come to pass in a different place with different people in my life. This would happen even to the extent of seeing buildings that had not yet been built or roads that did not yet exist; or, I now realize, people and animals that had not yet been born and were not even in this life yet. The people I would see mostly indistinctly in a setting were people I could not possibly know because they lived in another place hundreds or thousands of miles away! What did all of this say about time and the course of events in my life? All of this was very frightening to me, but I kept at it.

The biggest problem was how to explain that I was seeing things maybe ten to fifteen years before they were created. I would see myself in a house that had not been built on land that had not been purchased by a person who was still a child. I would see an adult woman in her thirties taking my picture in a very specific setting who, at the time that I had the vision, was only a young woman in her teens. I was seeing future events not only in my life, but where they intersected with events in other people's lives far in the future. To look closely at all of this made me feel like the ground was not only shaking beneath my feet, but that it was evaporating! These were times when it was very difficult to maintain a solid grasp on everyday reality. I could only stand to think about all of this for short periods of time.

I zeroed in on the issue of whether something that I saw, which might be natural scenery and buildings, maybe buses in a city street, a street in a town, a bridge, could already somehow exist when I saw it years before. However, in order for a déjà vu experience to occur, the season must be exactly correct, the time of day as well, the people present must be assembled, the exact words must be uttered at exactly the right time, and so on. All of this would be extremely difficult to arrange as anyone who has tried to make a movie would attest. It is nearly impossible just to get five people to meet somewhere at a certain time! A déjà vu scene is very specific. Everything has to come together, every detail, in order for it to be recognized. I have often been amazed that I could remember such things from so many years past, but I do. So it clearly was impossible that what I had seen way in the past actually existed when I saw it. I was seeing things that were going to occur I knew not where and I knew not when.

Occasionally, I would be present in a setting where a déjà vu occurred for some time before it happened to me. The setting was there, but the correct combination of people, words, light, events under way, time of day or night, etc., had not yet occurred. Therefore, the only conclusion I could draw was that I had seen things that had not yet come into existence. Even though certain elements of what I saw may have already existed, such as mountains, plains, rivers, and buildings, the particular circumstances in which I saw these things had not yet occurred. Déjà vu can, however, occur to a person in the process of watching a movie or reading a book. It is possible to have dreams or visions of scenes that occur later in movies or in the imagination while reading a book. The shock can be produced by a certain phrase that someone utters that we see every day or every week in our present life, but who may not have been present in our life when we had the vision; or if they were present, they had a different appearance. As was said earlier, déjà vu is very specific with respect to the circumstances in which the recognition occurs.

The next problem that I had to confront was that, if these complex events involving people, places, and things had not ever happened, what exactly was I experiencing when they did happen? In other words, what was the role of the senses in everyday experience? How could I experience an event in a dream state where I "saw," "heard," "smelled," or "felt" something that did not exist; and how, then, did I experience the same things with the same senses when they did occur in due time as my life evolved? Finally, what was the nature of everyday experienced reality? All of these questions have been slowly answered over time, but the one conclusion I soon came to was that when I saw the vision that I would later recognize as déjà vu, that is, already seen, I was seeing into the future of my life and the lives of others who would be with me. I was seeing elements of my life plan.

At the time that I would have these visions, there was no way that I could understand them, because my life at that time was completely different. I had no context into which I could situate the circumstances or people of my original vision in order to understand it. If I was living in a flat land, how could I relate to an event that occurred in rugged mountain country? If I was single, how could I understand something that was to happen to me as the parent of a large family and all in a split second? Then there was the problem of separating life experiences from events in a book, a movie, or a play or television. All of this was not only baffling, it was overwhelming to the point that I was left wondering what it all meant. All that was certain was that when these events, with all of their complexity of time and space, actually came to pass before my eyes or in my mind's eye in the case of a book, I was dead certain that I had seen it all before, and sometimes I was pretty sure when it was and where I was at the time I saw it.

Many déjà vu experiences brought a strong impact because of their uniqueness or the repetitive nature of the visions. In two cases that I can recall, the only way the scene that had been pictured in my memory earlier could be seen was through a very narrow field of vision. In one case, I kept having a vision of some kind of bridge partially visible in the distance. Some time later, I rented a house located on a bluff high above a small town. The town was situated in a horseshoe bend in a river and was an old railroad town. When I rented the two-story house, I climbed to a bathroom on the second story, which had a small window. It was only about two feet square. As I looked out through this small window, I could just make out, through an opening in the trees and over the rooftops of the town, part of a railroad bridge that crossed over the river. It was exactly as I had seen it in my dreams! I was definitely stunned. My heart stopped for a moment. I needed to go to this window many times and look out on that scene many times in order to believe what I was seeing.

In the second instance, which I now realize was similar to the first, I had repeatedly envisioned a winter scene where I was looking down on what appeared to be a streetlight with snow pouring through the light it cast. Once again, I rented a house on a mountainside above a small town. It was summer when I moved in. Later that winter, I noticed that, without the leaves on the trees, I could see a small gas station on a street corner at the bottom of the mountain. Still I made no connection with my dream visions until early one morning, I looked down on the gas station and saw snow pouring through the light that illuminated it and the whole street corner below me. It was not enough that I knew that the station was located several streets down the mountain from my new home, and it was not enough that I could even see the gas station and the street corner after the leaves fell. The picture was not complete until heavy snow poured through the whole scene making a white cascade in the blackness of the night. These experiences were so specific, so unique in time, place, and setting, that I took them to be reassurance that, however chaotic my life seemed to me, I was where I was supposed to be. It was a strange comfort. Because I moved about so much and because, despite my best intentions, I was estranged from my family, I had few of the reinforcing elements in life that remind us of who we are and why we are somewhere. These visions made me feel that someone or something was looking out for me, as I lived out my life plan, and was sending me messages of support.

Some visions would appear to me repeatedly. I began to get the idea that what I would see repeatedly was of especial importance and foretold significant changes in my life. However, because I had no context into which to place the elements of the vision, I had no way to tell really what I was seeing. Many times when these visions would appear to me, I would have some consuming emotional focus, such as where I would live next or if I would have a job or who I would be with. It was impossible not to color my interpretation of the visions with these emotions and concerns. Years later when the actual scene would occur in my life, my circumstances were so radically changed that it was clear that I could never have even come close to understanding my visions at the time they appeared to me. More recently, it has become clear that some things appeared to me over and over because that is what would happen. For instance, I would repeatedly see a certain street or see myself moving along a certain road in various seasons or different times of the day. It turned out that the street was where someone lived who would become very important to me. When the time came for it to happen, I would go down that street every day. The road that I repeatedly saw was not even built when I saw it! However, I travel that road all the time now.

Under what circumstances do the déjà vu scenes originally appear to me? What is the difference between a vision and a dream that will later be recognized as déjà vu? There is very little difference. Sometimes déjà vu scenes will originally appear in my mind as part of a dream, but I am unable to tell which scenes in the dream are predictive and which are simply part of the dream. Sometimes scenes and visions will pass through my mind as I drift off to sleep or am just waking up from sleep. These visions occur in that Proustian half-asleep/half-awake state that gave rise to three or four volumes of narrative for him. I am now pretty sure that what I see in this semi-somnolent state are in fact visions of future events, but I cannot tell what they are about or what they mean.

In one instance, I did know what the visions meant, but I found it very disturbing and tried to forget about it. One morning when I was waking up in the room that I rented from a family in southern France, I saw a jumble of faces of women and short episodes of their lives. I saw a series of different women and different life settings. I was in my early twenties and was uncommitted romantically. For various reasons, I had not had much luck forming strong bonds with women, but I clung to the ideal of one true love for a lifetime. Somehow, in my groggy, half-awake state of mind, I knew that this series of faces and snippets of lives was my matrimonial future. I sensed that this vision was telling me that I would have many wives with all of the turmoil and heartache that it implies. I was very upset with this vision and drove it into the back of my mind until after my first wife committed suicide, my second wife abandoned me and my son, and I was in the midst of a divorce with a third. Fortunately, this is all over now. So, at the point when I was just starting out in life, still in the midst of completing my college education and clinging to an ideal of marriage that rejected the possibility of divorce, I was shown that ahead of me was a course of events that would be contrary to my ideals.

Can these visions be called up or requested from the universe? I have been able to go into a sort of meditative state and see some things which have guided me in my activities. I was once prompted to seek employment in New England because I would see fields lined with stone walls and broad valleys full of color. I succeeded in finding employment in a New England state, although my time there was far from ideal.

Some déjà vu events happen very shortly after the scenes occur to me. At the time, what I see is innocuous, seemingly meaningless, but when it actually occurs in "real" life, it still has an impact. Recently, I had visions of standing before a class directing instruction. Since I am a teacher, there was certainly nothing unusual about that. When the scenes emerged from reality as déjà vu events, they stunned me to the point where I felt like I was spun around where I stood. I experienced a moment of disorientation and loss of control. No one in the classroom seemed to notice anything. In these moments, time seems to stand still or even roll back for a few seconds. In any case, it stops having any meaning. When I got home that day, I told my wife that something was going to happen because I had had two strong déjà vu experiences in a row that day. Within a few days or weeks of that experience, I gathered together various facts and figures and decided to retire! This decision, however logical it seemed at the time, was completely unexpected to me. I had no intention of retiring. Once I had a dream of being in a small room with various people, and I had a very bad feeling. Months later I was in a small room with the administrators of the community college where I was teaching, and I was informed that my teaching position was being eliminated. I know that the dream made very little impression upon me at the time and that I did not remember recognizing anyone. It was simply one of many scenes that passed through my mind at that time. When the actual meeting did occur, I definitely remembered the dream. This is one of the frustrating aspects of precognitive visions. Without an experiential and emotional context, a particular scene has very little meaning. It might just be something that happens in a book that I read later, a movie I watch, or a story someone is telling.

There can be another type of precognitive vision that is not specific at all, but very general in nature. At different times in my teaching years, I would "see" the faces of my future students and colleagues flow through my mind. I knew at that time exactly what was going on. I knew that I was being shown the faces one after the other, very rapidly, of all of those who would be in my classrooms later. From this experience, I learned that my students had signed up for my classes long ago before they were born and that I could indeed respect their presence in my classes and my time with them. What occurred in my classes came to have a whole new meaning.

Some scenes in dreams and visions are the result of a "bleed through" from another life in another time. This may be a parallel life that is occurring at about the same time as this one, or it may be a life that has occurred in the past but is recalled by present activities. We do things in this life that are influenced by or that influence other lives in other settings. When I was taking courses to improve my Spanish, I had dreams in which I was dressed like a Jesuit missionary priest leading along a group of Indian children in a hot dusty setting somewhere in the Americas. I have also occasionally seen scenes of a parallel life in the United States in a time around 1950 or 1960 when there had never been a world war or a Korean War. Visions of this type are discussed in other books at length, but it is necessary to be familiar with them in order to understand some things that may happen in our dreams and visions.

Visions may happen, however, in broad daylight while we are doing something else. During a particularly troubling time in my life, I would walk along a shady street in the town where I was living in order to escape from the turmoil in my home. As I walked, a beautiful, kind face would appear just above my forehead. This would happen over and over. Eventually I would see this face from memory, and I could recall it any time I wanted. I suspected that this face was the face of someone that I would know in better times, but I was in a conflict as to how to receive this information. At the time, I was unhappily married to someone, but I did not want to see another marriage end. It did end. Several years later the person whose face I had seen was my wife in another place far away from where I was when I would see her face in visions. Even though we may be granted visions of solace in hard times, we may not be morally or emotionally willing to accept them. Another such vision happened not in broad daylight, but in the dark of night. A few times when I was driving down the interstate in New England at night far from any city, momentarily in my windshield would appear a lighted boulevard with a green median, passing light fixtures, traffic, and various buildings of an apartment complex. Many months later, I was driving at night down the boulevard that passed by the apartment complex where my family then lived in a southern state. I was shocked to realize that this was the vision I had had in New England. I do not know how many times I had driven down that boulevard at night before the realization hit, but certainly it was quite a few times. The other times were just not exactly right, I guess. What I always wondered after the vision appeared in my windshield in New England was how long did I roll along the interstate with the city street in my purview, and what or who was guiding me down the interstate?

Often in times of struggle and conflict, it was very helpful to recall various things that I had seen in order to give myself the comfort and reassurance that something was going to happen that presumably was a change for the better. Since we have lessons to learn from what we struggle with in life, what may be better may simply be a greater challenge. I had become such a desperate person that I feared that I would not even survive, so visions of a future life gave me hope and got me up and going on to the next task.

I have occasionally seen things in visions that actually prompted me to action in order to bring about what I had seen. This was especially the case once, when I seemed to have reached an impasse in my life and seemed to be going nowhere. Because of visions of stone walls, colorful foliage, snowy scenery, and ski slopes, I actually began making calls to New England and quickly set up many job interviews there, which resulted in a job. This time in New England, however, proved to be very challenging to the extent that I had a stroke! So I certainly went from having no job to having a job somewhere else, but the visions did not necessarily lead to "better" times or a "better life."

Sometimes it may not be anything visual at all that moves me to action. It may be a hunch or a feeling that I have in my chest. In one troubling time, I was passing through a neighboring city, and I was drawn to a shopping center that was closing down. I did not really know what I was looking for, only that I was supposed to investigate the failing shopping mall. Once in the mall, I came upon a tiny bookstore and found a very comforting and reassuring book that I still refer to frequently.

Since we plan our life, it is useful to follow the guidance that helps us to live out our plan. Of course, we must be aware that there is guidance, and we must be willing to accept and interpret it. This acceptance, however, may require us to think in ways that are not considered acceptable by the rules of "rational" Western civilization. First of all we used to be accustomed to taking all such promptings, feelings, dreams, or urgings to a priest figure for evaluation and interpretation. Your average person was not expected to be able to understand such things for themselves. This, of course, put all such things in the hands of the priests and church institutions. Anyone who set out on their own to find explanations risked having the label "witch" or "devil" attached to them with the attendant consequences.

Now we live in a materialistic world where science and technology are the new authorities. Anything that is not subject to scientific proof is not considered valid. Anything that is said to exist outside of the five senses is subject to disapproving skepticism. In other times, in other places, information that came from nonmaterial sources or extra-sensorial sources was accepted as viable information to be considered along with sensorial information. Yet, we live in a world where miracles happen every day around us. People are born into our lives and they die. New creatures are born and die. There are plants where there were none. People are healed surprisingly, and people die for no apparent reason. Plenty of things happen irrationally and uncontrollably, and we accept this as natural. It is time that we expand our acceptance of the irrational and uncontrollable to include sensory and mental experiences that defy explanation in everyday terms. There is clearly a lot more to living than strictly material experience.

Chapter 8
Choices

What would it be like if we were to choose to look at everything in our life as if it were created by us with heavenly assistance just for our edification and advancement? What if we were to see everything as help on our way to spiritual maturity, to advancement toward new capabilities? If we expected the arrival of all of our children as if it were previously agreed upon in heaven, how would we relate to them? It is often said by people who have been in life-threatening situations that they were overcome with a strange sense of calm, a sense of reassurance. This is often the last thing they remember before they wake up in a hospital. Does this feeling come from the strong idea that what is happening to them is a preplanned part of their life?

What if we were taught from an early age that all those we came upon in our life were there to help us advance toward God and we them? Further, what if we saw those around us as familiar souls from heaven? We like to talk about soul mates nowadays, but what about soul friends? What if we were to greet everyone we came upon with the attitude that we asked him or her to come into our life to help us?

Our modern communication systems now unite us in ways never before possible. It is now quite possible to suffer with and to have sympathy for the struggles of people all over the world. It is now even possible for us to see their suffering or joy wherever in the world they may be. These same people contribute to our everyday life because they all contribute to the manufacture of the things we use in our lives, and we make the things that make their lives better. We are all in this together. We know this and are reminded of it more and more every day, but we forget that everyone who is on Earth now is cooperating with us to make our life come out the way that we planned it. We are doing the same for them. To do this, we are in constant communication with them, even though we do not know it consciously. If we were not in communication with them, then how could so many things that we need and expect happen when we need them to happen? When we are grateful, we acknowledge this mutual cooperation and give it more power to help us and others. When we are grateful, we choose to be aware that we live in a cooperative universe that is helpful to us and to everyone else. This makes everyone more capable of achieving his or her goals.

Living in the Earth is all about such choices. We are confronted with choices at every moment. Each time that we create our material world, we are challenged to choose to do the right thing and approach God or not. As explained earlier, our material environment then disintegrates and instantly reforms so that it includes the effects of beliefs and decisions of the previous choice. Now we are challenged to make a new positive choice again; then, the phenomenal gestalt that we have created for ourselves with much help from God, heaven, our friends, neighbors, relatives, and spirit guides is reformed before our senses and our life progresses accordingly. Not to choose is the same thing as to choose not to affirm the divine beneficence of our Creator and our creation. Not to choose is to deny our divine being, but our world recreates itself automatically with this denial as part of its makeup. We are now, in this example, living in a world for an instant with our enjoyment of God's grace diminished. In the next instant this can change. It is all according to the choices we make every living moment of our conscious life. When we sleep, we get a break from this rhythm.

What we actually create from moment to moment depends in large part on what our life plan has been. That we have such a plan is evident in the checkups and reassurances that come from near-death experiences and déjà vu moments, among others. There are plenty of accounts of people who have a near-death experience or who have seen their whole life flash before their eyes in times of extreme stress. Many people who thought that they were dying only to find that ultimately they returned to life, recount that they went before a group of heavenly counselors that came forward to review their life with them. Often they describe having their life shown to them on a sort of screen. Some people have similar experiences in dreams. They are encouraged by their counselors who have appeared for this purpose to compare the way things have gone with the way they had been planned. Naturally, there is a decision to try to do better.

Implicit in all of these descriptions are another world to which we repair somehow for a review of our life; benevolent, loving counselors who are intimately familiar with us and our life; and a prearranged life plan that involves not only us individually, but all of those who live in our life with us. Every individual has a life plan; every family has a life plan, and so do every community and nation. Even the Earth has a life plan. Also implicit in these reviews of our life is the presence of senses, emotions, rational thinking, and comprehensible language. It must be kept in mind that all of these descriptions of our spiritual encounters are a very simplified narrative of a much more complex event that involves levels of experience and consciousness that are incomprehensible to us in terms of our earthly life. That is to say, there is much more to life than these explanations, but we conduct ourselves according to the explanations that we understand. This is all that we need right now.

When we come upon a déjà vu experience, then we also check in with our life plan as it was previewed for us at some earlier time. It is inevitable that questions of preordained versus free will will arise, but there is less of a problem here than it seems. We set out to live our life in a certain place and time in earthly existence because that suits our purposes for moral and spiritual advancement. We choose our family, and they agree to accommodate us. We choose our various occupations, travels, if any, spouses, children, neighbors, friends, coworkers; and they choose to fulfill these roles for us. Obviously this can get complicated. What is not complicated at all is the choice that we are challenged to make in all of this between divine beneficence and our own power to be versus stagnation and retrogression. We advance or we do not; it is that simple.

Of course if it were that simple, there would probably be no need for such complex creations. For someone like me who was raised with the idea of the inherent malevolence of life and everything in it and with the idea that I was totally inadequate to the task of succeeding in this hostile world, it is not so simple. I am sure that many people have been imbued with other similarly crippling beliefs. Then, there are the beliefs that we may pick up along the way, such as that one sex is inferior to the other or that people who have chosen a different life plan are inferior or superior to us. We may have come to believe that the best way to live our life is to turn our mind over to a controlling chemical or some controlling person or organization of people. Anything is possible as a challenge either to choose our divine power and divine assistance or to choose to be fixed upon the fleeting material manifestations of our power. Matter disintegrates instantly and must be constantly reconstructed. Divine power is eternal.

If we are indeed the ones who are creating our life in each instant, then how can that life be inherently hostile to us? It can be if we create it that way and believe that what we are creating is that way. There are plenty of others who would help us with such beliefs. We have a large part of our religious authorities all over the world, regardless of what name is given to their claim to authority, who relentlessly sell us on the idea that the world is an evil place full of evil influences and evil people, etc. Our political organizations want it to be that those "others" are purveyors of evil. Then there are many people who are going around and around in circles in pursuit of the same earthly pleasure over and over again, and who invite us to join them in their pursuits. It is not difficult to find beliefs of a hostile world. Such beliefs are also found in layers and layers of beliefs that have practically taken the form of national traditions. The belief that the world, however we may create it, is hostile is necessary to those who wish to create the illusion of the control of existence. If the world is evil and hostile, they argue, then we need to let them manage it for us, and so on and so forth. This illusion of control then leads to the outward manifestation of material wealth. People who think that they are in control need to have a lot of material possessions and wealth to show off their power. A great deal of energy must be devoted to maintain and preserve all of this wealth. Others covet this material wealth because they do not think that they can make their own, and conflict ensues.

Another set of beliefs that go along with the conviction of powerlessness is that it is the role of others to provide all things for us. Such beliefs require us not to aspire to accomplishments, not to assert our God-given abilities, and to believe that no one else should either because it makes us look and feel bad.

Historically, our Western ideas of creation have been that God made the world and that we had no hand in it. From that, it followed that our role was to passively, resignedly accept the world as it is and seek the assistance of those in authority, whether religious or political, in dealing with it. This God that created the world was like our father and we were his children. This relationship was stagnant, however, because everyone knows that children grow up and get in your face! Children grow up rapidly and, as they do, they are expected to take over more and more responsibility in the daily life of their family and ultimately of their community. Children are also extensions of their parentage. They naturally resemble the parentage from which they sprang. If this is the way of nature, then it follows that the divine children of the paternalistic Godhead would become creators like him. This part has been left out of our Western thinking, and it is obviously an important part. Fortunately, this is not part of all religious thinking around the world.

In many cultures that have lived very closely with nature and about which we in modern times know a thing or two, such as the ancient Greeks, Egyptians, the ancient tribes of Europe, and modern aboriginal peoples, all things in nature were considered to have life and spirit. Not only did all things have spirit, but in many instances their spirit also had a name. We see this tendency to name natural spirits and even the spirits of manmade objects in the medieval practice of naming swords, shields, houses, furniture, etc. Native American artisans speak of the spirit of their creations. Jewelry must have an opening somewhere so that its spirit may escape; patterns of decoration must provide for the spirit of that pattern. Old European cultures, ancient Mediterranean cultures, and Oriental cultures have many names for wood nymphs, water sprites, forces of nature, elves, fairies, goblins, jinns, etc. For us, a wind from the west is just that; for the Ancient Greeks, it was Zephyr. All of this is to show that creation is not some fixed lifeless thing with which we must cope as best we can, but that many people see creation as very much alive, participating in our life with us. Everything is animated in a way with divine spirit so much so that this spirit can be named. The creations in nature are here to enjoy and reflect divine beneficence and to help us learn and progress on our way to God. Nature is therefore an expression in material form of God in all things. We all participate in its creation at every moment. We allow pets to come into our lives, and we love them. How much different is it to allow the wind, trees, flowers, and other plants (even poison ivy) into our life with our blessing. Our blessings may also extend to water, Earth, rocks, and concrete, maybe even plastic.

Many more millions of people over the course of human history have enjoyed this perception of natural creation than have isolated God in a temple or house of worship. Such beliefs about nature have been disparaged in the name of polytheism. Of course, it is not so easy for a priest to control someone's beliefs in divinity that is scattered over the fields, mountains, and rivers. It is much easier to control belief in a God that is contained in representations under one roof or in a box. Further, if you do not happen to have such a roof or such a box where you live, too bad for you until we bring you one! Then there is the conflict over whose roof and box is the proper, authentic one worthy of worship.

To depart from such limiting ideas allows us to indeed celebrate all creation in all of its aspects and see it as the material expression of the Holy Spirit. We may now welcome nature and all life as positive and helpful. A positive attitude makes all things possible. A negative attitude imposes limits where there are none.

This is not a world where anything goes, however, because in the world of heavenly consciousness, in that spiritual world that brings about our material one, there are indeed many controls. The curious thing is that we know very little about them. Even if we knew more about them, we could understand very little. We know from near-death narratives and reports from mediums and readers of the Akashic records, that we have counselors who help us organize our life plan. We now know that we have guides who help us live out our plan. We know that there is a lot of talk about angels and archangels who assist with life events when called upon but remain distant from earthly existence. We do hear about a divine plan for Earth which is mentioned piecemeal in Holy Scripture and about which we know only that the purpose of all life is to create a world that better reflects God's will for us. We are pretty certain that God's will is not to perpetually blow up everybody and everything. It is certain that positive, constructive help is available. We need to choose to see it and use it.

We need to see that we are all united in our path toward God. Behind our everyday material reality there is all of the telepathic interaction that helps create and maintain our reality. Souls and ideas far removed from us in time and space provide us with the information to create our world, and the souls of our relatives, friends, and neighbors participate with us in the creation of our life. Whether we like it or not, we are not alone in our daily life. To profit from all of this influence with a grateful positive attitude not only will enhance our prosperity, but it also will lift up everybody everywhere.

Earlier in chapters 2 and 3, it was explained that our soul is like a television tube with a cathode that shoots out electrons onto a phosphorescent screen. Our soul projects energy onto the Earth environment, which forms matter so that our physical senses may record it and register all of it as an experienced moment of reality. It is like a star whose energy is focused in the time and place where we are living. Our soul expresses itself in the Earth as matter. We have many sources of help in how we create our matter at any one time. Help not only comes from those other souls who are here on the Earth with us at this time, but it comes also from those who have already been in earthly life who have left a legacy of ideas from which we may draw. And help comes from what could be described as layers of divine guidance in the spiritual world.

To return to the near-death experience reports, one common activity of those who seem to go over to the non-Earth side of life is a review of their life plan with a group of counselors who offer encouragement. These counselors are very familiar with our life plan, our life story, and its course. They helped us organize it in the first place before we entered Earth.

So there are controls. A person only comes into Earth life after a plan for their life has been organized. Sylvia Brown's guide, Francine, even gives an estimate of how long this takes in Earth years. Everyone who is to participate in the life of this person has to agree to fulfill his or her role, which may include being cruel or what seems cruel to us. Despite how it seems, not everything is allowed, however. If there were not some bad, we would not strive to eliminate it. Also, what is to happen in a particular life has to fit in with the customs, history, and conditions of the times. This can be quite complex and cannot be fully explained. The choices that we make now in our life form what these customs and conditions will be that future generations will have to conform to in their life plan. After World War II, the existentialists, particularly Jean Paul Sartre, put forth the idea that we are each responsible for what it means to be human. Our individual choices in each moment that we create with others show what human life is and in what direction it is going. This is a sobering prospect.

If we want certain behavior such as political repression or child abuse and exploitation removed from the human experience, or if we want education for all, then we need to make these choices now. Once these choices have been made, then they are made for all of those who are yet to be born. We can begin now by actively rejecting or encouraging these things, mentally, every day in every thought we have, in our conversations and in our various life decisions. This is to say that we can adopt a bit of a realistic Pollyanna attitude that the world must not include what is harmful, and when possible act in such a way that no energy is given to acknowledging or supporting some things. Some examples might be that we would not attend certain movies, attend to certain forms of entertainment, refuse to speak lightly or jokingly about things that are abhorrent, etc. These are things that many people now do anyway.

The main thrust of this thinking is the abandonment of the more traditional Western belief that the world is made for us by some power over which we have no control. Of course, we will turn around and say that we believe in free will and freedom to choose without acknowledging the apparent contradiction in our beliefs. We make our world at each instant just like a basketball player makes the strategy and action of the game at each second of play. How can any basketball player say in the middle of the game, "I just woke up this morning and they had the ball and were dribbling down the court toward their basket?" The coach would obviously object to such thinking at any point in the game!

Before we were born, we each agreed to create a certain life course. Hundreds or thousands of others agreed to support our plan and be where we wanted them to be and do what we wanted them to do when we wanted them to do it. We made the same pact with them. We agreed to be where they wanted us to be and do what they wanted. It is complicated, but obviously it works. We are all doing these things and a lot more every day as we go about our life. We are doing it all and we are responsible. No one would stand up and say that World War II just happened. Millions of people did or did not do millions of things over time that led us to the war. We could certainly say that millions of people went to work to bring it to an end. About this there are innumerable personal stories and thousands of books and history courses.

Along with the belief that we have no hand in making our world, goes the possibility that then God is responsible. Is God responsible for the death camps and slums? After World War II, many said that, indeed, God was responsible. The God of creation is responsible for killing and mayhem? Is this God Moloch or Shiva? When we neglect our responsibilities to one another and to our life purpose to do for others what we want them to do for us, then it certainly appears that God is responsible for mayhem. A train can be driven recklessly and neglectfully off its tracks. Did this just happen, or did the crew of the train have a hand in it? We delight in telling stories about someone who is faced with dire circumstances and who prays and for whom others pray, and then they are spared the undesired consequences of their circumstances. We cite these instances of the power of prayer and reaffirm our faith. In such instances we rightly assert that our faith and wishes indeed changed the course of events in our life and someone else's life.

The trouble is that we see these instances as extraordinary. We do not imagine that they may be quite ordinary and everyday, but, then, why not? Does the God of destruction and mayhem provide for special windows of opportunity for such dire, threatening circumstances? Many times I have wondered if this was ultimately our thinking. According to our beliefs, the world is made for us, but is unmanageable without the intervention of our divine teacher—namely, Jesus, Mohammed, Buddha, Krishna, Moses, or some other. But in special circumstances, we may put our wishes and intentions together in prayer and bring about changes and outcomes ourselves. Which way is it? I have always wondered.

Why can it not be that the same God or divine source that brings about our existence as we wished in order to exercise our free will to choose the beneficence and grace of that God would support the choices that we make? The other way has God running at counter purposes to creation. God creates you in a world that will destroy you unless you ask for something otherwise. Even this contradictory picture of the world allows for us to have the power to change the course of things. We are at each moment creating for ourselves, and ultimately for everyone with whom we share our life, a world of our own making as a consequence of our beliefs and attitudes. At each instant of our creation we can change what that world is. These changes may happen gradually or rapidly. This is the path to a better world!

Chapter 9

If There Is a New Earth, Is There a New Heaven?

If there is a new Earth in which mankind is much more involved with creation and more aware of this involvement, then correspondingly in heaven are spiritual entities much more involved with creation as well? It should be easy to recall that in the Middle Ages and in the Dark Ages before that, the Church was in control of everything it was possible to control. Above all the Church controlled thought. No thoughts contrary to Church doctrine were tolerated. If anyone had such thoughts, they had best keep them to themselves. Things were not much different in the Muslim world. In the day-to-day world only priests were allowed to have much in the way of spiritual thoughts or ideas and, of course, these were strictly in line with Church doctrine. It was all about control. Anyone who deviated very much ran the risk of being first tortured, then burned at the stake if they survived. For the spiritual world to provide promptings, urgings, or dreams to those in the physical world was to invite disaster. Was the Church, thus at war with heaven itself? Clearly it was.

The Church also controlled all scientific knowledge; or, since the word "science" then only meant knowledge, the Church controlled all thinking as to the nature of reality, of the stars, of history, and of the universe. Ninety-nine percent of the people were illiterate, so they had no way of knowing anything any different. Also people did not live very long, maybe thirty to forty years in good times; so heaven was very busy ushering souls in and out of existence. Obviously fewer people desired to incarnate, and populations were much smaller than in our time. Survival was never very far from everyone's mind. Undoubtedly divine protection and divine intervention were often required to sustain human life. Overall, however, the prevailing idea was that this life on Earth was subservient to the one to come in heaven and only the Church could provide safe passage to a proper place in heaven. Overall there was an attitude of hostility toward life itself, toward creation, and toward anything that might interfere with the authority of the Church. The joy, liberation, love, and enlightenment of spiritual knowledge could only be acknowledged in the strict terms of Catholicism. It was

75

not unlike what we see in the Muslim world today, which is passing through the same stages as Catholicism has. This hostile, unfriendly atmosphere tied the hands, so to speak, of the spiritual world and limited its influence and effects in this world. Of course we now still carry this fear and hostility around in us toward all thoughts not properly sanctioned by political and religious authority. Some would simply call this the fear of God, and perhaps they would be right.

In Europe, the Roman Catholic Church overreached in its corruption and attempts to control ideas. Its authority was challenged by Renaissance ideas, by the Reformation, and by the invention of the printing press. Also the papacy, having no army capable of challenging the kings of European lands, had to tolerate royal rebellion. Creation itself finally got the best of Roman Catholic domination because these kings sent out ships to find new routes to the Spice Islands. The usual routes were closed by the Muslims. These ships discovered lands forgotten for thousands of years. These lands were inhabited by previously unknown beasts and people. Catholics asked the Church authorities if these beasts had been part of the Garden of Eden as well; and if so, how had they survived the flood on the other side of the ocean far away from Noah's ark? And the people, were they of the lost tribes of Israel? Did they have souls? Were they to be respected as children of God? Then, along with new lands and new people, fossils were discovered of still more fantastic beasts. It was all too much to control.

Priestly authority and dominance of thought was certainly not solely the way of Catholicism. A similar authoritarianism was behind the power of priests and shamans in other parts of the world during the European Age of Exploration (1400–1600). While the Mayas, Aztecs, and many other non-European cultures practiced human sacrifice, the Roman Catholics practiced immolation as acts of faith. Ultimately religious practice, with many notable exceptions, was in constant opposition to any positive or benevolent influences from the world of spirit. Hence, we have spirit and evil spirit. To be fair, these were certainly not the best of times for human existence on the Earth, and religious beliefs and attitudes reflected this state of affairs.

On the one hand, the spiritual world had to cope with a belief system that was off message and that expected hostility from the gods and from nature. On the other hand, human affairs were directed toward eventual world unity and reconciliation. Now the nefarious beliefs of dominant religious cultures are on the wane despite how things appear at times. The way is now clear for heaven to be heard by humankind once again. Clearly it is being heard because we make blindingly rapid material and spiritual progress in our time.

So many material manifestations bear witness to the renewed accessibility of the spiritual world that exists just "behind" the veil of reality. The break with how things seemed to be in the medieval past is that obviously the spiritual sources of all of our creation can now be enjoyed by everyone in the modern world. This new open relationship is evident in TV programs that discuss guides, communication with relatives that are no longer present in the material world, remote healing, and spiritual sources for understanding modern events, such as Edgar Cayce provided us. It would be wrong to declare that the spiritual world or heaven is more willing to communicate with those in the material existence. That willingness has never been abated. It is that now beliefs are changing and our new changed beliefs allow overt responses to communications with the other side. We can discuss such things, as is being done here in this and so many other books, without fear of torture and death. There may be social consequences, but that is possible for any number of ideas. Recently, I was reminded of the very words of the Declaration of Independence that all "are endowed by their creator with the right to life, liberty, and the pursuit of happiness." This is certainly not a medieval idea. This is a modern belief. This is a very positive idea about the purpose of life. It states that the source of our life in this world expects us to pursue living our lives to the fullest in freedom and prosperity.

As above, so below. Obviously the universe is unlimited in its power to create. Why should our life in the material world of three-dimensionally directed energy be limited? We come to this life from the unlimited spiritual realm, and when we are finished with this episode in our consciousness, we return to that realm. It is on both ends of our existence here. It is in the background while we are here. Why should the spiritual background to existence be denied or excluded from our ideas about it? When we say the Lord's Prayer, we say, "Thy will be done on earth as well as in heaven." Do we mean it? How can we not mean it? Whenever we say this we need to look for how this is being played out and ask for instructions as to how to best implement this will.

Direct and immediate access to the spiritual source of our being can be experienced by the following mental acts:

1. Mentally or literally list all the things that we have to be grateful for individually and collectively.

2. Ask questions about anything in our life that is puzzling to us, anything.

3. Begin expecting an answer to come to us in some form or another.

4. Pay attention to our inner voices, urges, and promptings to do or say something that may be beneficial to ourselves or others.

5. Do to others what you would have them do for you. (It's not for nothing that this saying has been around for thousands of years.)

6. Keep in mind that when solutions to your problems appear, *all* problems and obstacles will be removed—even the things that we never imagined would be problems or obstacles. We will not have to get up and do all of the things we imagine we will have to do. The way will be made clear. We only have to act with confidence.

Obviously there is nothing new in any of this. What is most important, however, is that anyone who is doing these things is actively engaged with their spiritual sources of power and knowledge. Once this engagement occurs, there is less and less the sense that you are all alone here and that you need someone's help. Once you begin these thoughts, your awareness changes and you will see a whole new world before your eyes. If you become distracted, you can begin again any time. These resources are always with you.

So will you hear voices? Maybe. Everyone has different antennae for this sort of thing. A hunch may come in the form of a tingling in the big toe, a feeling in the elbow, an itch in the nose. Who knows? Promptings can vary according to circumstances. Pay attention! Most of our problems arise from the fact that we are not paying attention. Can we strike out boldly on our own without being sure? What do we do every day?

We need spiritual maturity to match our creative maturity. We need to recognize the rapid advances made in spiritual awareness that correspond to the rapid advances in material creation. In other words, it is time that we realize that, in fact, we are capable of all of the things that we have done in the last two hundred or so years and that, therefore, we are indeed a new kind of spiritual being on the Earth—all of us.

What great progress might we make if we accepted our spiritual powers now? Clearly, new forms of communication would emerge and new forms of healing as well. Why couldn't investigations and research open up in these areas beyond what is now being done furtively and in severely limited attempts? If more and more people are in communication with the world beyond this material world, what kinds of things might they know that could help all of us? We must emerge from medieval thinking and understand that rather than being ancient, occult knowledge, spiritual, intuitive knowledge is obviously the most modern form of knowledge yet known. It is, in fact, the veritable source for all of our new gadgets.

This knowledge allows us to look at life in a positive way. We can understand that on many levels we are creating everything that happens in our life including changes in the shape and structure of the Earth itself. We are the ones who bring about the life plan of the Earth in our time. We can see that everything that happens with all of the attendant participants was planned way in advance, and everyone volunteered to be here with us to make it all happen. We likewise volunteered to help everyone else with his or her life plan. We are all in this together no matter where we happen to live on the Earth. We are constantly in communication with each other about what is happening and what we intend to happen. We are also in communication with all of those levels of spiritual reality that assist our creation and regulate the events in our life that are part of a greater divine plan. Hence, we are not just participating in our life and the lives of our family and friends, but we are helping to bring about a divine plan on a much broader scale. In Christian terms, we are all bringing about the Kingdom of God on Earth and in heaven in every small decision we make at any moment. Each time that we choose the positive, each time we choose to create something better for ourselves and others, we are helping to create God's plan for the Earth.

Afterword

In many cases the point of departure of some other inform-ants on these subjects is similar to mine. Seth, for instance, talks about telepathy among individuals and implies that it is more extensive, but he does not expand the idea to the ex-tent that my sources do. Seth also explains that the reality that we perceive with our senses is created by us and is part of our consciousness. He suggests that the television analogy is ap-propriate for explaining the way that our brains create the ma-terial reality before us and that that reality is a reflection of our beliefs. My sources apply the television cathode ray tube anal-ogy to approximately describe how the soul creates the body and the reality around the body.

Seth is the one voice that convinced me to begin examining my beliefs extensively. I am grateful for his exhortations. I found this examination to be difficult going. I felt like a person who has to find a place to stand while he tears down his house. In my book I wanted to give my readers some ideas on where to start in examining their beliefs as well as ideas on the conse-quences of having certain beliefs. I wanted to provide a place for them to start that would be easier than not knowing where to start at all.

Now, Seth is a channeled source of information similar to my sources. Both sources are speaking from beyond everyday ma-terial existence, but from the reality that lies behind that mate-rial existence. It is comforting that there is consistency in the explanations of both sources. The same consistency can be found in other sources that describe the spiritual background to our practical reality. Our problem really is that for too long we have chosen to ignore and disparage this information de-spite the fact that it has such consistency. This choice has de-prived us of valuable possibilities for personal development.

I strongly encourage everyone to read the Seth material from the 1960s and 1970s. It can be found on the Internet under that title. The NDE or near-death-experience site is also one that will provide a lot of interesting information. We should each follow our own path to explore what it is that is important to us at this time.

Appendix 1

The Go-to-Heaven Workshop

We all go to heaven regularly subconsciously when we sleep, when we daydream, when we have quiet, vacant moments, or when we are idle or just thinking. Some people may be aware that their consciousness has slipped past the veil of energy that separates us from heaven, but most are not. Moreover, we are taught by our religious authorities that heaven is a forbidden place of stern judgment and that it is the alternative to the dreaded hell.

Of course, innocent babies come to us from heaven and we send our loved ones there when they die, so it must not be so forbidding. Besides we also believe that heaven is the abode of angels who help us out of love and concern. This workshop is meant to teach people that they may easily go to heaven consciously any time that they want and benefit from the assistance that they may find there.

In order to do this meditation you need a "special place" which you may visualize. This should be an imagined place where you feel at ease and secure. It could be at the beach, in the mountains, in your back yard, in your grandmother's kitchen or on her porch. Any place that you can think of where you feel calm and secure from the day's demands will serve our purpose. You must design this special place with some furniture. There should be places for four or five people to sit down in a circle. If your special place is on the water or in the air, you must still provide room for "guests."

Next, you need to think of two, three, or maybe five or six people who can meet with you in your special place for a few minutes. These may include people who are now with you in your life or people who have moved on or people who have passed on. You may ask Jesus of Nazareth or an angel or any other such religious figure to join you as well. When I do this workshop with groups, it is called *The Love Your Guides Workshop*. It is also a workshop to introduce people to their spiritual guides, so you need to ask your guides to come and join your group in your special place. The idea of having spiritual guides may be new to you, but just go along with this and see what turns up.

One of the other things this workshop is about is learning to ask questions and wonder about things. The whole universe, God and everybody else, is here to help us live our life and we need to learn to ask for information. We need to ask for answers to life's mysteries. We need to wonder out loud. The guides continually remind us that they cannot help us if we do not ask. At the beginning of the workshop, I ask everyone to write down at least three questions that they would like to have answered. I want to see how many of these questions are answered even before the workshop is over. These questions are the beginning of our dialogue with our higher powers and spiritual development. You also need to have a question or two to ask your assembled guests when you join them in your special place.

Now that you have imagined a special place, have selected several souls to join you there, and have prepared several questions to ask them as well as a few for the universe, it is time to begin our journey to heaven. I usually take people through some guided visualizations to exercise their imaginations. We are able to communicate with the spiritual world through our imagination, so it is important to be receptive and accepting of whatever we imagine. For practice, you can imagine standing at the end of an airport runway and watching and listening as a jet takes off overhead. This is a multiple-sensory experience that is good to stimulate the imagination. Do not forget to imagine the vibration of the air and ground when the plane is overhead. Another such sensory imagining could be walking along the bottom of a swimming pool in water that goes from our ankles to our chest and then turning around and going back out to the shallow end.

Finally, I ask everybody to imagine a pond in the woods complete with sunlight dappling the water, frogs croaking, birds chirping, and a gentle breeze. After a minute of this image everybody needs to imagine a foggy scene with a tall doorway with double French doors that arches up above their heads. They are to step up to this mist-shrouded doorway, push down on the door handles, and push the doors open before them. Then step into the scene on the other side.

Here, you see ahead of you in the lifting fog, a sunny scene with a dirt path that leads along between intensely green meadows.

Maybe there is a rail fence along one side. These green meadows go rolling off in the distance. There may be animals in the meadows. Maybe there are black-and-white Holstein cows of intense shades of black and white, almost shimmering. Maybe there are other kinds of cows or horses or other animals. There may be cats and dogs, maybe some beloved pets, maybe ducks or chickens or whatever meets your fancy. There may appear people who seem to float along over the bright green grass. Some will wear brilliant white robes; others will be dressed in various fashions. They may smile and nod to you as you stroll along the winding path. You may begin to feel enveloped in a warm, loving vibration that will go all through you and stay with you. This is the heavenly feeling of unconditional love. It is a very strong and undeniable feeling. Up ahead you will see a grove of tall trees where the path splits off into three or four directions. On a hill above and beyond the trees you will see a sort of temple or white marble building with Greek columns on a porch at the top of a dozen steps. When you reach the grove of trees where the path divides, you need to step off along the path that leads to your special place. You will automatically know which is the right path. The feeling of warm embracing love will go with you.

Once you move along this path a while, you will come to your special place with your invited friends and relatives there waiting for you. There may be some emotional greetings. You should thank them for agreeing to join you here, and then you should ask one or several of them some of your questions, but not too many at first. Then you must wait quietly and listen to what they have to say in answer to your questions. It might help to have some way to scribble some notes about what you hear them say. Your guides are standing on the sidelines and after you have absorbed what the souls of your friends and relatives have said to you, invite your guides to step into the circle where you can see them. In some cases there may be only one guide at first.

Guides may be dressed in all kinds of outfits, depending upon how they want you to recognize them. They may be giants or they may be short. They can be from any time, any place. Rather than appearing in human form, your guide or guides may appear as a glowing ball of white light. These heavenly forms will speak and respond to you affectionately nevertheless. Greet your guides and thank them for choosing to guide you through your life and for joining you in your special place. Ask them some questions. Listen carefully to what they have to say. Among your questions should be the names of your guides. Here you may have difficulty understanding because the names may come from strange languages from far back in time. You and your guides can work out what you want to call them. If you are new to the idea of guides, you and they may have a lengthy conversation. Just let it all flow through your mind and do not resist any thoughts for any reason or in any way. This takes practice and discipline, so you may have to begin with short and simple messages. If you are surprised by what you learn, wait a while and in the days and weeks that come you will find confirmation for what you have learned.

Now you may think of going back down the path from whence you came. Thank everybody once again for joining you here and say good-bye. You may walk out between the intensely green meadows toward the tall, arched doors standing open the way you left them. This time, after you step through the doorway, you may want to leave the doors open to symbolize the free access you have to this special place. The next time that you want to go there in your imagination, you may go directly to your special place or you may want to proceed through the doorway and walk along through the green meadows.

It could be useful to keep some notes about what you learn and you may find that you are somehow guided in what you write. Do not resist. Do not reject. At first what you write may not make a lot of sense to you. Be patient and in time all will become clear. You may find that when you finally grasp what you have been told, you will be stunned by it all for a while. This will not be knowledge that everybody has. It will not fit in with what we are taught in our culture, and knowing it will begin to change how you see things in your life. Knowing these things may invite other new information into your experience. Always remember to be grateful for the assistance that you receive and articulate your gratitude to your guides, to the universe, and especially to God. From this gratitude will come great benefits to you and to all about you.

Appendix 2

A Note about Hell

Rob Bell in his book *Love Wins* suggests that the threat of being condemned to a place of fire and smoke inhabited by humanoids with horns and long tails is inconsistent with the loving, caring message of Jesus of Nazareth. This suggestion started a lively discussion among theologians revolving around the semantics of Bible translation and Hebrew traditions. We have a much better way to test the question of whether there is such a place in the universe or not.*

Today there are many counselors of people seeking help for life's problems who practice hypnotic regression. The patients are hypnotized and asked about their past lives. A recording is made. Thousands of such recordings have been made. Sylvia Brown, Dolores Cannon, Dr. Michael Newton, and Dr. Brian Weiss are a few of those who have perfected this counseling technique and have published many books where they report their findings. This has been going on now for more than twenty years. Patients not only talk about their past lives on Earth, but also past lives in other places in the universe. They discuss their time between lives and what they must do in heaven to prepare for their next earthly life. There are many descriptions of what heaven is like, but no place like the hell described above anywhere ever.

Then, we have near-death-experience reports, some of which have recently appeared as bestselling books. Five years ago there was only one Website on the Internet devoted to NDEs. Now there are three with hundreds if not thousands of reports. Never is there mention of anything like the hell of our religious teachings.

We have many spiritual counselors who have published books about how they have helped people by contacting departed relatives and friends on the other side. Often these books describe searches that are made throughout heaven to find the soul of a departed loved one. The descriptions of heaven are consistent: there is a strong feeling of unconditional love; there are temples and green pastures; there are pets; there are many souls engaged in various activities similar to what we do on Earth. There is never any mention of hell. We can watch these mediums work on television programs. I have yet to hear one say to a client, "I am sorry, but your dear departed uncle is in hell and we can't talk to him."

We can now read books by people who have had various types of out-of-body experiences. There is a great variety to their experiences, but no mention of a place of fire, smoke, and devils with tridents and tails. In fact, when we are asleep, when we daydream, when we are lulled into a semiconscious state by boredom or monotony, we often visit heaven or some place between heaven and Earth. Like the NDE survivors, we mostly do not remember these brief departures from our Earth life. Some people even accomplish great works during these departures from Earth consciousness, but I have never heard of anybody describing an assignment to hell.

Not only is there no hell, but heaven itself is not an exclusive and forbidden place. After all, we all accept that this is where the souls of babies come from, and we understand that babies and young children are fresh visitors from heaven. Heaven is our home even when we are involved in a life elsewhere. Our spirits are alien to the material world and do not participate directly in it. Really the chemical reaction that is fire is a property of matter. Heat is a human sensation related to the tactile senses of the body. The soul is unrelated to these things. It is in a realm far beyond the behavior of the molecules of matter.

If a person wants to experience hell, they may travel to North Korea or to Syria, for instance. They could go live in the poorer sections of large cities. They could spend time in a family where people are mentally or physically abused or where there is addiction to something. These are states of existence where there seems to be a separation from the awareness of divine grace. This separation is only temporary and is brought about by erroneous beliefs. These beliefs can affect how heaven and spiritual states are experienced. In other words, the beliefs that lead people to be in difficult situations in their life on Earth will go with them to the afterlife and carry along the same feelings of difficulty. In this way it is possible for people to create their own personal hell. There is no shortage of spiritual help for this, however.

We can now know a great deal about heaven, and we can visit there whenever we want, but pretty much no one has ever described a psychic experience like the hell of Dante's *Inferno*, or like the Renaissance paintings of Hieronymus Bosch, or like the colorful descriptions of some of our religious institutions and their representatives. In heaven, and really on Earth, we can have whatever we want. We can be wherever we want to be. The hell of Western religions is certainly something that we could create somewhere for our own personal purposes if we wanted to.

This section is adapted from an article called "Hell? No." first published in the April 2014 issue of Oracle 20-20 magazine.

About the Author

When he was a sophomore in high school, L. R. Sumpter first read Ignatius Donnelly's book on Atlantis. This was the beginning of a lifelong interest in "maverick" history and science. This interest continued over years of formal study for undergraduate and graduate degrees. These studies reached the doctoral level and have been done in eight universities on two continents and in four Western languages. This interest has not diminished through more than thirty-five years of teaching in elementary, secondary, and higher education settings.

L. R. Sumpter has also worked for many years in engineering and sales. He has lived and traveled in forty-eight of the fifty states in the United States and ten foreign countries. He has taught, written articles for publication, and presented papers in two languages. Finally, after retiring from teaching it has been possible for him to devote full time to studying and writing about unorthodox topics.

Dolores Cannon
A Soul Remembers Hiroshima
Between Death and Life
Conversations with Nostradamus,
    Volume I, II, III
The Convoluted Universe -Book One,
    Two, Three, Four, Five
The Custodians
Five Lives Remembered
Jesus and the Essenes
Keepers of the Garden
Legacy from the Stars
The Legend of Starcrash
The Search for Hidden Sacred Knowledge
They Walked with Jesus
The Three Waves of Volunteers and the
    New Earth
Aron Abrahamsen
Holiday in Heaven
Out of the Archives – Earth Changes
Justine Alessi & M. E. McMillan
Rebirth of the Oracle
Kathryn/Patrick Andries
Naked In Public
Kathryn Andries
The Big Desire
Dream Doctor
Soul Choices: Six Paths to Find Your Life
    Purpose
Soul Choices: Six Paths to Fulfilling
    Relationships
Tom Arbino
You Were Destined to be Together
Rev. Keith Bender
The Despiritualized Church
O.T. Bonnett, M.D./Greg Satre
Reincarnation: The View from Eternity
What I Learned After Medical School
Why Healing Happens
Julia Cannon
Soul Speak – The Language of Your Body
Ronald Chapman
Seeing True
Albert Cheung
The Emperor's Stargate
Jack Churchward
Lifting the Veil on the Lost Continent of Mu
The Stone Tablets of Mu
Sherri Cortland
Guide Group Fridays
Raising Our Vibrations for the New Age
Spiritual Tool Box
Windows of Opportunity
Cinnamon Crow
Chakra Zodiac Healing Oracle
Teen Oracle
Michael Dennis
Morning Coffee with God

God's Many Mansions
Claire Doyle Beland
Luck Doesn't Happen by Chance
Jodi Felice
The Enchanted Garden
Max Flindt/Otto Binder
Mankind: Children of the Stars
Arun & Sunanda Gandhi
The Forgotten Woman
Maiya & Geoff Gray-Cobb
Angels -The Guardians of Your Destiny
Seeds of the Soul
Julia Hanson
Awakening To Your Creation
Donald L. Hicks
The Divinity Factor
Anita Holmes
Twidders
Antoinette Lee Howard
Journey Through Fear
Vara Humphreys
The Science of Knowledge
Victoria Hunt
Kiss the Wind
James H. Kent
Past Life Memories As A Confederate
    Soldier
Mandeep Khera
Why?
Dorothy Leon
Is Jehovah An E.T
Mary Letorney
Discover The Universe Within You
Sture Lönnerstrand
I Have Lived Before
Irene Lucas
Thirty Miracles in Thirty Days
Susan Mack & Natalia Krawetz
My Teachers Wear Fur Coats
Patrick McNamara
Beauty and the Priest
Maureen McGill
Baby It's You
Maureen McGill & Nola Davis
Live From the Other Side
Henry Michaelson
And Jesus Said – A Conversation
Dennis Milner
Kosmos
Guy Needler
Avoiding Karma
Beyond the Source – Book 1, Book 2
The History of God
The Origin Speaks
James Nussbaumer
The Master of Everything
Sherry O'Brian
Peaks and Valleys

Other Books By Ozark Mountain Publishing, LLC

For more information about any of the above titles, soon to be released titles,
or other items in our catalog, write, phone or visit our website:
PO Box 754, Huntsville, AR 72740
479-738-2348/800-935-0045
www.ozarkmt.com